CW01670258

HOW TO CRACK THE CODING INTERVIEW FUN?

Useful Book of Python Programming Questions and Answers

Oliver Morgan

Table of contents

I'm delighted you've chosen my book **"How to Crack the Coding Interview Fun?"**. We appreciate your interest in this comprehensive guide that will equip you with the necessary knowledge and skills to excel in Python interviews.

In today's competitive job market, being well-prepared and confident when facing Python interviews is crucial. Whether you are a fresher looking to kickstart your career or an experienced professional seeking to enhance your Python skills, this book is designed to be your go-to resource.

This book will give you valuable insights into the most commonly asked Python interview questions, detailed answers, and explanations. The content is carefully curated to cover various topics, including fundamental Python concepts, object-oriented programming, and more.

The experience you will gain from reading this book goes beyond just providing you with answers. It will empower you to develop a deeper understanding of Python and its applications, enabling you to tackle interview questions with confidence and clarity. You will learn essential programming techniques, best practices, and industry-relevant tips to set you apart from other candidates.

Furthermore, this book emphasizes a practical approach, offering real-world examples and scenarios to help you apply your knowledge effectively. You will find coding exercises and solutions that encourage hands-on learning, allowing you to sharpen your problem-solving skills and reinforce your understanding of Python concepts.

Whether you are preparing for a technical interview, aiming to enhance your Python expertise, or seeking to refresh your knowledge, **"How to Crack the Coding Interview Fun?"** serves as your reliable companion throughout the journey.

We are confident that by immersing yourself in the contents of this book, you will gain the necessary confidence, knowledge, and skills to ace Python interviews and excel in your career. So, dive in, explore the chapters, and embark on a transformative learning experience that will pave the way for your success in the dynamic world of Python development.

Thank you once again for choosing our book. We wish you an enjoyable and rewarding journey as you delve into Python interview preparation.

Oliver

Introduction

Welcome to **"How to Crack the Coding Interview Fun?"**, your practical guide to mastering Python for interviews and beyond. Whether you're a beginner looking to break into the world of programming or an experienced coder aiming to brush up on your Python skills, this book is designed to help you succeed in interviews and develop a deeper understanding of this versatile language.

Python is one of the most popular programming languages, known for its simplicity and readability. It's used in various fields, including web development, data analysis, artificial intelligence, and more. If you're preparing for a Python-related interview, we've got you covered.

What to expect:

- In this book, we'll provide you with 200+ interview questions and answers that are carefully curated to cover a wide range of Python topics.
- We'll emphasize practical examples to ensure you not only grasp the concepts but can apply them effectively.
- Our aim is to help you understand the core principles, syntax, and best practices in Python, which will make you a more confident and skilled Python developer.
- Remember that interviews aren't just about getting the right answer; they're about demonstrating your problem-solving skills and your ability to communicate your thought process.

What to pay attention to:

- Focus on the logical reasoning behind each answer. Understanding why something works is often more important than memorizing it.
- If you're a beginner, don't be discouraged by challenging questions. Start with the basics and work your way up. Python is a language that rewards perseverance.

Useful tips:

- Practice, practice, practice! The more you code, the more confident you'll become. Don't hesitate to create your projects to apply what you learn.
- Stay up to date with the latest Python trends and libraries. The tech world is constantly evolving, and staying current will give you a competitive edge.
- Don't be afraid to seek help from online resources, forums, or communities when stuck. Python has a vibrant and supportive community.

Remember, Python is all about problem-solving and creativity. Embrace the challenges and enjoy the journey of becoming a proficient Python developer. So, let's dive in and start cracking those Python interview questions!

Why you need to prepare for an interview?

In today's competitive job market, aspiring software developers and programmers must stay ahead of the curve. Python, one of the most popular programming languages, has gained significant prominence recently. Python has become a go-to language for many applications with its simplicity, versatility, and widespread adoption.

When it comes to interviews for Python-related positions, whether you are a fresher or an experienced professional, thorough preparation is crucial. Here are a few reasons why you need to prepare for an interview in Python:

Industry demand

Python is extensively used in various domains, including web development, data science, machine learning, artificial intelligence, and automation. As a result, there is a high demand for Python developers in the job market. By preparing for a Python interview, you enhance your chances of securing a desirable position in a competitive industry.

Core language concepts

Python interviews often assess your understanding of core language concepts. This includes topics such as data types, variables, control flow, loops, functions, object-oriented programming, and exception handling. Preparing for these concepts ensures that you have a solid foundation in Python and can confidently tackle interview questions related to them.

Problem-solving abilities

Python interviews typically include coding exercises or problem-solving questions. These aim to evaluate your ability to apply Python concepts to real-world scenarios and develop efficient solutions. By practicing problem-solving and coding exercises, you sharpen your skills and develop a systematic approach to tackling complex programming challenges.

Frameworks and libraries

Python boasts an extensive ecosystem of frameworks and libraries that facilitate rapid development in various domains. Familiarity with popular Python frameworks, such as Django and Flask, and libraries like NumPy, Pandas, and TensorFlow can significantly boost your profile. Interviewers often assess your knowledge of these tools and expect you to demonstrate hands-on experience during the interview.

Best practices and coding standards

Employers value candidates who adhere to best practices and coding standards while writing Python code. Understanding concepts such as code readability, modularization, documentation, and version control is vital. By familiarizing yourself with these practices, you demonstrate professionalism and dedication to producing clean and maintainable code.

Preparing for a Python interview helps you showcase your skills and knowledge and boosts your confidence. It lets you articulate your thoughts clearly and concisely during the interview, increasing your chances of impressing the interviewer and securing the job.

In **"How to Crack the Coding Interview Fun?"** we delve deeper into various topics and comprehensively cover the most commonly asked interview questions. Whether you are a fresher starting your career or an experienced professional looking to improve your Python skills, this book is an invaluable resource to help you succeed in your Python interviews.

Remember, preparation is key. Invest time and effort in studying Python concepts, practicing coding exercises, and familiarizing yourself with industry best practices. By doing so, you will be well-equipped to confidently tackle any Python interview and increase your chances of landing your dream job.

How to crack your Python developer interview?

Follow these steps for success:

STEP 1: MASTER DATA STRUCTURES AND ALGORITHMS

Ensure you can compare Python data structures with abstract ones. For instance, understand how to implement stack features using Python lists or create a custom linked list. Be familiar with lists, dictionaries, tuples, and group construction.

Practice a custom linked list implementation using an internal class called Element (or Node) to manage data elements.

STEP 2: CODE PROFICIENCY ON PAPER OR WHITEBOARD

Comfortably write Python code on paper or a whiteboard, as interviews may not involve a computer. Demonstrate understanding of loops, control flow models, list comprehensions, and basic classes. Fundamental coding skills are a must.

Practice coding without a computer; it's a common scenario in interviews.

STEP 3: SHOWCASE HOBBY PROJECTS

Share code from personal projects to prove your coding abilities. Whether it's a web interface, data processing script, or a small desktop program, demonstrate well-organized and idiomatic code. Host projects on GitHub, BitBucket, or GitLab for visibility.

Make your projects public to showcase your coding style and proficiency.

STEP 4: UNDERSTAND FRONT-END TECHNOLOGIES

While not mandatory, having a basic understanding of front-end technologies like HTML5, CSS3, and JavaScript is valuable. Collaboration with the front-end team is common, so familiarity with their work enhances your versatility.

Explore front-end technologies to better collaborate with the development team.

STEP 5: PROBLEM-SOLVING SKILLS

Differentiate yourself with strong problem-solving and analytical skills. Listen carefully to requirements, ask relevant questions, and convert problems into code. These skills are crucial for handling complex scenarios in a Python developer role.

Practice problem-solving scenarios to sharpen your analytical skills.

STEP 6: BASICS OF OTHER TECHNOLOGIES

Stay open to learning new technologies beyond Python. Familiarity with technologies like JavaScript, CSS, Java, etc., demonstrates your adaptability and willingness to learn, enhancing your long-term employability.

Stay updated on emerging technologies to broaden your skill set.

Do's and Don'ts of Python Developer Job Interview

Do's:

- Understand the control flow of Python.
- Use list comprehension.
- Grasp Object-Oriented Programming concepts.
- Familiarize yourself with the use of generators.
- Practice coding on paper or a whiteboard.
- Be prepared to explain each line of code.

Don'ts:

- Avoid excessive cramming before the interview.
- Embrace coding questions from the interviewer.
- Avoid arguing with the interviewer; express your thoughts respectfully.
- Don't memorize code; focus on understanding.
- Stay confident and avoid nervousness.
- Be polite in all situations.

We hope this guide helps you prepare for your Python developer interview. Follow these steps, keep practicing, and remember to stay calm and confident. Good luck!

Who am I?

Welcome to the exciting world of Python, where creativity and problem-solving intertwine. If you've been searching for Python resources, rest assured you're not alone. The internet is bursting with information, which can be overwhelming, especially if you're starting. That's why I'm here. In this book, I'll provide you with the most common questions and answers you might encounter during your search to land your dream job.

I'm Oliver Morgan, a Python enthusiast with over two decades of experience in software development. While I am an accomplished Python programmer today, my journey began a decade ago, sparked by a deep interest in video games. I was driven to tinker with and modify the games I loved, so I took the plunge and started experimenting with code. It all began with a minor adjustment, but when I witnessed the game responding to my changes, it ignited my passion.

From there, I delved deeper into programming, exploring concepts like logic and variables and experimenting with programming languages like C and Perl. However, these languages often left me frustrated and on the brink of giving up. That's when I stumbled upon Python, a burgeoning language with immense potential. Conceived initially as a labor of love by a single developer, Python rapidly gained popularity and attracted a community of programmers who refined and expanded it into the elegant and efficient language we know today.

Within just a few months of immersing myself in Python, I experienced a profound "aha!" moment. Python's simplicity and versatility left me astounded. It allowed me to concentrate on problem-solving rather than becoming entangled in complex syntax. I began transitioning my existing code to Python and never looked back. Python's portability and clean structure became my steadfast allies in crafting software for various applications, from web development to innovative side projects that pushed the boundaries of my creativity.

Now, I'm delighted to share some of the most intriguing questions you might face in an interview. I have a knack for translating intricate ideas into plain, understandable terms. This is precisely why I penned this book – to assist you in securing your dream job.

This book will encompass theoretical and practical questions ranging from challenging to straightforward. Together, we'll prepare for any Python interview. I'll provide clear explanations, practical examples, valuable tips, key takeaways, and potential pitfalls to ensure you can quickly grasp everything.

Let's prepare for your interview together and pave the way toward that dream job.

How can this book help you?

The book **"How to Crack the Coding Interview Fun?"** can be a valuable resource to help you prepare for Python-related job interviews. Here's how the book can assist you:

Comprehensive coverage
The book contains a curated list of 200+ Python interview questions that cover a wide range of topics and difficulty levels. This comprehensive coverage ensures that you get exposure to various aspects of Python, making you well-prepared for a variety of interview scenarios.

Interviewer's perspective
The questions in the book are often structured to reflect what interviewers frequently ask candidates during Python job interviews. By practicing these questions, you will become familiar with the types of problems and challenges that commonly come up during interviews.

Answer explanations
Each question in the book is accompanied by a detailed answer explanation. This feature is invaluable because it not only gives you the correct solution but also helps you understand the reasoning behind it. Understanding the logic and thought process behind each answer can enhance your problem-solving skills.

Python concepts refresher
Whether you are a beginner or an experienced Python developer, going through these interview questions will serve as an excellent refresher on various Python concepts, data structures, algorithms, and coding techniques.

Building confidence
As you practice answering the questions and gain a deeper understanding of Python, you'll become more confident in your abilities. This newfound confidence will positively impact your performance during the actual interview.

Preventing surprises
The book's content is curated based on common interview patterns, so you'll be less likely to be surprised by unusual or unexpected questions during the interview.

Practical Experience
The more you practice answering interview questions, the better you'll become at solving problems quickly and efficiently. This practical experience will translate into better performance during your real interview.

Performance under pressure

Job interviews can be nerve-wracking experiences, and practicing with this book can help you become more comfortable solving problems under pressure.

Personal assessment

By attempting the questions and comparing your answers with the provided explanations, you can assess your own strengths and weaknesses in Python programming. This self-awareness will enable you to focus on areas that need improvement.

Remember that the book is a supplementary resource, and it's essential to combine it with other study materials, projects, and hands-on coding practice to build a well-rounded skill set for Python development. Additionally, improving your communication and problem-solving skills will also be crucial for performing well in any job interview.

How can You help this book?

Dear reader, I've put my heart and soul into creating this book as your ultimate guide to mastering Python interview questions. My aim is to make your interview preparation journey both enjoyable and stress-free.

Now, I need your assistance in spreading the word and helping fellow programmers on their quest to secure their dream jobs and interviews. Leaving a review on Amazon would be a tremendous favor that can genuinely impact others. Your feedback not only inspires me to produce more valuable content but also assists others in discovering this invaluable resource.

Leaving a review is a simple process! Just scan the QR code provided, and it will take you directly to the review page.

However, if recording videos isn't your preference, fret not! A written review expressing what you found valuable about the book holds equal significance.

Remember, there's no obligation to leave a review, but your contribution can truly make a positive impact in the world and pave the way for others using this book.

Thank you for embarking on this incredible journey with me. Together, let's unlock the doors to Python programming success!

Python Basics

1. What is Python?

Python is a fantastic programming language that was first brought to life in 1991 by a visionary named Guido van Rossum. It's a high-level, general-purpose language that puts a strong emphasis on code readability and offers an incredibly user-friendly syntax. This means that writing and understanding Python code is a breeze, especially for beginners like you!

One of the reasons why Python has won the hearts of so many developers and programmers is its simplicity. It's like a friendly and reliable companion that makes the journey into the coding world enjoyable and less daunting.

Fast forward 30 years, and Python is still going strong, continuously evolving with the support of an active community. In 2018, Guido van Rossum stepped down as the leader of the Python community, passing the torch to other talented developers to carry on the legacy.

2. Why Python?

Python is a fantastic high-level, general-purpose programming language that opens up a world of possibilities for you. What does "high-level" mean? Well, it means Python lets you focus on the essential functionality of your application while taking care of routine programming tasks behind the scenes. This makes your coding journey smoother and more enjoyable!

Python's versatility is another reason to love it. You can use it to create all sorts of things, from user-friendly desktop GUI apps to dynamic websites and powerful online applications. Whether you are interested in data analysis, web development, or even scientific computing, Python has your back!

One of the most incredible things about Python is its readability. The language has a clean and straightforward syntax, so you can easily understand and maintain your codebase. This is helpful when working on more extensive projects or collaborating with other developers.

3. Why is Python so popular?

Python's popularity goes beyond just being beginner-friendly. It's available on various operating systems, making it versatile and accessible to a wide range of users. The reference implementation of Python, known as CPython, is open-source, meaning that its source code is freely available for anyone to view, modify, and contribute to.

Speaking of community, the Python Software Foundation, a non-profit organization, takes care of Python and CPython. This community-based development model ensures that Python stays vibrant and continuously improves with each passing day.

4. How to install Python with Anaconda?

Head over to Anaconda.org: Go to Anaconda's website and click on the "Download Anaconda" button. This will lead you to the download page.

Get the latest version: Once you're on the download page, you'll see the latest version of Python available for download. Just click the download button, and you're all set.

Installing Python: Now, depending on your operating system, follow the installation wizard instructions. It's pretty straightforward and user-friendly. Anaconda will take care of everything for you.

Power up your IDE: After Python and Anaconda are installed, it's time to choose an Integrated Development Environment (IDE) to write your Python code. There are plenty of options out there, such as Visual Studio Code, PyCharm, or Jupyter Notebook. Pick the one you like the most and get ready to code!

Start coding in Python: With Python and your favorite IDE ready to go, you can now start exploring the world of Python programming. Don't worry if you're a beginner; we all start somewhere! There are fantastic resources online, like Python tutorials and beginner-friendly courses, that can guide you through the process.

If you're looking for more guidance, I recommend checking out some Python tutorials. They can be incredibly helpful in getting you up to speed with the language and its syntax. And, of course, practice makes perfect, so don't hesitate to start writing some small Python programs to get hands-on experience.

5. What are the applications of Python?

Web Applications

Python is perfect for building web applications. With libraries like Django, Flask, and more, you can create dynamic and interactive websites that cater to your users' needs.

Desktop GUI Applications

Do you want to build user-friendly applications with a graphical interface? Python's Tkinter library makes it easy to create intuitive and beautiful desktop applications.

Console-based Applications

Python's command-line prowess is well-known. With its Read-Eval-Print Loop (REPL), you can swiftly execute command-line programs and perform various tasks efficiently.

Software Development

Python is a reliable support language for software development. From build control with SCons to automated testing using Buildbot and Apache Gumps, Python has you covered.

Scientific and Numeric Computing

Embrace the world of artificial intelligence and machine learning with Python. Its scientific and numeric libraries, like NumPy, Pandas, and Scikit-learn, simplify complex computations.

Business Applications

Python offers scalability and readability, making it perfect for creating business applications. Check out Oddo, a Python-based application that provides a wide range of business solutions.

Audio and Video-based Applications

Python's versatility extends to multimedia applications. Build your own music or video player with Python using libraries like TimPlayer and cplay.

3D CAD Applications

Python can help you create 3D CAD applications if you're into engineering and architecture. Try Fandango, CAMVOX, or HeeksCNC for your next CAD project.

Enterprise Applications

Python is the go-to choice for developing applications within businesses and organizations. Take inspiration from real-time applications like OpenERP and Tryton.

Image Processing Applications

Explore the world of image processing with Python's powerful libraries like OpenCV, Pillow, and SimpleITK. Manipulate images to your heart's content.

6. What are the advantages of Python?

Easy to Learn and Use

Python's user-friendly design makes learning, reading, and writing a breeze. With its clean and straightforward syntax, you'll be coding like a pro in no time.

Abundance of Third-Party Modules

Python has a vast array of third-party modules extending its capabilities. Need to perform numerical calculations? NumPy has got you covered. Want to analyze data? Say hello to Pandas!

Active Community and Open Source

The Python community is a lively bunch! With countless developers contributing to its open-source nature, you'll find support, resources, and inspiration at every step of your coding journey.

Object-Oriented Programming

Python supports object-oriented programming, a powerful paradigm that helps you efficiently organize and manage your code.

Interactive and Portable

Python's interactive nature allows you to test code on the fly, making debugging a breeze. Plus, it's portable across different operating systems so that you can code anywhere!

Ideal for Prototyping

Building prototypes has never been easier. Python lets you quickly add features with minimal code, perfect for turning your ideas into reality.

High Performance and Efficiency

Don't be fooled by its simplicity - Python is a true workhorse! It offers high performance while allowing you to achieve more with less code than other languages like Java or C++.

Internet of Things (IoT) Possibilities

With Python's versatility, you can venture into the exciting world of IoT and bring your smart device ideas to life.

Extensive Library Support

Python's library repository is a treasure trove! You'll find libraries for almost any task you can imagine, making your coding projects a breeze.

Error Detection on the Fly

Python's interpreted nature checks each line of code as it runs, detecting errors early on and making debugging a less daunting task.

Free and Open-Source

The best things in life are free, and Python is no exception! You can use Python without any cost and enjoy the support of the generous open-source community.

Concise and Expressive

Python's beauty lies in its simplicity. It allows you to accomplish a lot with fewer lines of code, saving you time and effort.

7. What are the key features of Python?

Python has gained immense popularity among data scientists and AIML professionals for its versatility and user-friendly nature. Let's dive into the key features that make Python a top choice for programming:

Easy to Learn

Python boasts a clear syntax and readability, making it a breeze for beginners to grasp. Its simplicity allows newcomers to focus on learning programming concepts rather than getting caught up in complex syntax.

Easy to Interpret

Debugging is made easier with Python's interpreted nature. Developers can quickly identify and fix errors, saving valuable time and effort.

Free and Open-Source

Python is freely available for anyone to use, modify, and distribute. This not only makes it accessible to everyone but also fosters a vibrant community that contributes to its continuous improvement.

Language Integration

Python plays well with other programming languages. It can be seamlessly integrated with languages like C++, Java, and more. This flexibility allows developers to leverage existing code and resources while benefiting from Python's powerful features.

Object-Oriented

Python supports object-oriented programming, which enables the creation and manipulation of reusable code blocks called classes. This paradigm promotes modular design and helps developers build scalable and maintainable applications.

Cross-Platform Compatibility

Python is compatible with various operating systems, including Windows, macOS, and Linux. This cross-platform support ensures that your Python programs can run smoothly on different devices and environments.

Rich Standard Library

Python provides a vast standard library, offering many modules and functions for common programming tasks. These ready-to-use resources save developers time and effort by providing pre-built solutions to common challenges.

Strong Community and Ecosystem

Python boasts a thriving community of developers, which means you'll never be short of support and resources. Online forums, tutorials, and open-source projects create a dynamic ecosystem fostering collaboration and growth

8. What do you mean by Python literals?

Let's dive into the world of Python literals – a fundamental concept in programming that allows us to express values simply and directly. Imagine literals as the building blocks of Python, representing different data types. In Python, we have various types of literals that you'll come across frequently.

String Literals

Strings are sequences of characters enclosed in single (''), double (""), or triple (''' ''') quotes. For example, "hello" or 'Python'. If you need to represent a single character, you can also use single or double quotes.

Numeric Literals

Numeric literals deal with numbers and are divided into three types:

- **Integer Literals:** These are whole numbers, like 0, 1, -2, or 100.
- **Float Literals:** Floats represent decimal numbers, such as 3.14 or -0.5.
- **Complex Literals:** Complex literals consist of a real and imaginary part, written as a + bj, where a and b are numbers, and j represents the imaginary unit.

Boolean Literals

Booleans are used to represent truth values. In Python, we have two boolean literals: True and False, which correspond to '1' and '0' respectively.

Special Literals

Special literals are used to represent values that haven't been generated yet. In Python, we use the keyword 'None' to denote such values.

Besides these, there are other types of literals you might encounter as you progress in Python:

Unicode Literals

Unicode literals allow you to work with Unicode characters and are represented with a 'u' prefix, such as u"hello".

List Literals

Lists are collections of items enclosed in square brackets ([]). For example, [], [5, 6, 7].

Tuple Literals

Tuples are similar to lists but are immutable, meaning they cannot be modified. They are represented with parentheses (()). Examples include (), (9,), or (8, 9, 0).

Dictionary Literals

Dictionaries are key-value pairs enclosed in curly braces ({}). Each key-value pair is separated by a colon (:), like {'x': 1}.

Set Literals

Sets are unordered collections of unique elements, represented by curly braces ({}). For instance, {8, 9, 10}.

9. What type of language is Python?

Python is a fantastic interpreted, interactive, and object-oriented programming language.

First, let's talk about being "interpreted." Unlike languages that need to be compiled into binary code before running, Python code is executed line-by-line by the interpreter. This means you can see the results of your code instantly, making it perfect for quick experimentation and learning.

Python is also dynamically typed, which might sound complex, but it's not! It simply means you don't have to declare variable types explicitly. The interpreter figures out the data types during runtime, making coding more flexible and user-friendly.

Now, onto Python's readability! One of its most beloved features is its concise and easy-to-learn syntax. This focus on readability means you can write clean code that is easy to understand, reducing software maintenance costs and making your programming journey more enjoyable.

But that's not all! Python comes equipped with classes, modules, and exceptions, allowing you to create organized and structured code. You'll also love its extensive standard library, offering a treasure trove of pre-built modules and packages for all kinds of tasks. This modularity and code reuse make Python a powerful tool for any aspiring programmer.

10. How is Python an interpreted language?

Well, it's all about how Python handles your code. When you write Python code, it doesn't get compiled directly into machine code like some other languages. Instead, Python takes a slightly different approach.

When you write Python code, you save it in a .py file. This is your source code, where all your brilliant ideas come to life. Now, here comes the magic: Python takes your source code and converts it into something called "bytecode." Think of bytecode as a set of instructions for a virtual machine.

This bytecode is created by compiling your .py source code into .pyc, which stands for Python bytecode. It's like a special language that Python speaks. Once the bytecode is generated, it can be interpreted by different implementations of Python, such as the standard CPython interpreter or PyPy's JIT (Just in Time compiler).

So, what exactly does the interpreter do? It's like a friendly guide for your computer's processor. The interpreter reads the bytecode and makes sure your code gets executed, variables get created as you specify, and everything runs smoothly. If there are any issues or errors, the interpreter will kindly point them out, helping you fix things along the way.

This unique approach of interpreting bytecode makes Python incredibly versatile. You can write your code on any platform, and as long as you have the Python interpreter installed, it can run on your computer. It's like having a universal translator for Python!

11. What is PEP-8?

PEP-8 stands for "**Python Enhancement Proposal 8**", and it's like a friendly guidebook for writing Python code. Think of it as a set of best practices and recommendations that help make your code more readable and consistent. Who wouldn't want that, right?

Back in 2001, a team of Python wizards, including Guido van Rossum, Barry Warsaw, and Nick

Coghlan, created PEP-8 to make Python code easier to understand and maintain. It's like having a roadmap to follow while you're on your coding adventure.

Now, you might wonder, what's this "**Python Enhancement Proposal**" thing? Well, Python Enhancement Proposals are like ideas or suggestions for improving Python. They cover all sorts of cool stuff, from new features to design and style elements. PEP-8 is just one of these proposals, focusing specifically on coding style.

So, why is PEP-8 essential for you? Well, imagine you're writing a story, and you want others to enjoy reading it, right? In the same way, when you write Python code, you want it to be easy for others (and your future self) to understand. PEP-8 helps you do exactly that!

By following the recommendations in PEP-8, you'll develop a clean and consistent coding style. It'll be like writing a beautiful poem with Python! Plus, when you start working on projects with other programmers, everyone will speak the same coding language, making teamwork a breeze.

12. What's a namespace in Python?

In Python, a namespace is like a naming system that gives a unique name to each object, whether it's a variable or a method. Think of it as a directory-file system structure in your computer. Just like you can have files with the same name in different folders, in Python, objects can have the same name in different namespaces.

Python keeps track of namespaces using a Python dictionary. Every name in your program is mapped to a corresponding object, creating a name-to-object mapping. This allows Python to ensure that all names in your code are distinct and can be used interchangeably.

You know how everything in Python is an object, right? Strings, lists, functions, and more – they are all objects. Python uses dictionaries to implement namespaces. The names act as keys, and the objects are the values in the dictionary.

Here are a few examples of namespaces:

Local Namespace
Created when a function is called and only exists until the function returns. It stores the local names of that function.

Global Namespace
Contains names from imported modules used in your project. This namespace is formed when the module is added to your project and lasts until your script is completed.

Built-in Namespace

This one holds the names of built-in functions and exceptions that come with Python.

Understanding namespaces is crucial because they help Python keep track of your objects, making sure there are no conflicts with names, and allowing you to use names across different parts of your code without any issues.

So, next time you hear about namespaces in Python, you'll know that they are like a well-organized system that ensures everything gets its unique name and place in the Python universe!

13. What is PYTHONPATH?

PYTHONPATH is like a magic portal that lets you add extra folders to Python's list of places to search for modules. Think of it as giving Python a treasure map to find all the special tools and resources you want to use in your code.

So, how does it work? Well, before Python starts running your code, it checks if there's a PYTHONPATH environment variable set. If there is, it adds all the folders listed in that variable to its search list. This way, Python can find your precious modules and packages, even if they're not in the default locations.

Let's break it down a bit more: Imagine you have a folder with some cool Python modules you want to use in your projects, but it's not in Python's usual search locations. By setting the PYTHONPATH to include that folder's path, you're telling Python, "Hey, don't forget to check this special place for tools I need!"

To set the PYTHONPATH, you don't need a magic wand; it's just a matter of adding the folder paths you want to include. You can do this either in your operating system's settings or through commands in your terminal or command prompt.

Now, you might wonder, why would I need to use PYTHONPATH? Well, it comes in handy when you're working on big projects or using third-party libraries. It allows you to organize your code better and keep everything neat and tidy. Plus, if you're collaborating with others, setting up a clear PYTHONPATH makes it easier for everyone to run the code without any fuss.

So, the next time you hear about PYTHONPATH, remember that it's a helpful little tool to extend Python's reach and make your programming life a bit smoother.

14. What are local variables and global variables in Python?

In Python, you might come across the terms "local variables" and "global variables."

Let's break down what they mean in a simple way!

Local Variables
Local variables are like secret agents that exist only within a specific function. When you create a variable inside a function, it becomes a local variable. Imagine it as a special agent that can only operate within that function and isn't accessible from outside. So, you can't use this variable beyond the function it belongs to.

Global Variables
On the other hand, global variables are like superheroes that have a presence throughout the entire program. These variables are defined outside any function and are available to every part of your code, both inside and outside functions. So, they have superpowers to be used across the whole program!

In a nutshell, local variables have a limited scope, confined to their function, while global variables have a broader scope, making them accessible all over your program.

15. What is a dynamically typed language?

Type checking is a fundamental aspect of programming languages, aiming to catch errors related to variable types. In the world of programming languages, we have two main categories: statically typed and dynamically typed. Here, we'll focus on dynamically typed languages.

Dynamically Typed Language Characteristics:
Type Binding at Runtime
In dynamically typed languages, the object's type is determined by assignments during runtime. This means that you don't need to specify the variable's type before using it. For instance, you can assign a string to a variable and later change it to an integer without any issues.

Optimization Considerations
Keep in mind that dynamically typed languages tend to produce less optimized code when compared to statically typed languages. This is because the type information is only known at runtime, making it harder for the compiler to perform certain optimizations.

Useful tip:

- While the flexibility of dynamically typed languages can be powerful, it's essential to write clear and well-documented code to avoid unexpected type-related bugs.

What to remember:

- In dynamically typed languages, flexibility is a key advantage. You can change variable types on the fly, which can be handy, but it also requires more rigorous testing to catch potential type-related issues that might only appear during runtime.

Program code:

```
# Python is a dynamically typed language
my_variable = 42  # This is an integer
my_variable = "Hello, World!"  # Now it's a string
my_variable = [1, 2, 3]  # And here, it's a list
```

In Python, you can see how the variable `**my_variable**` changes its type as we assign different values to it. This flexibility is a hallmark of dynamically typed languages. However, it also means that you need to be cautious to prevent unintended consequences in your code.

So, in a dynamically typed language, you have the freedom to assign and reassign variables without specifying their types in advance, but with great power comes great responsibility. Be mindful of potential type-related issues and always keep your code well-organized and documented.

16. What are keywords in Python?

Keywords in Python play a crucial role in defining the language's structure and syntax. These special reserved words serve as identifiers, function names, or variable names, and it's essential to understand their significance during interviews.

Here is a list of all the keywords you should be familiar with:

Keywords in Python:

False	await	else	import	pass	False	await
None	break	except	in	raise	None	break
True	class	finally	is	return	True	class
and	continue	for	lambda	try	and	continue
as	def	from	nonlocal	while	as	def

During your Python interview, having a good grasp of these keywords will demonstrate your understanding of Python's core concept.

17. What are comments and how can you add comments in Python?

In Python, comments are snippets of text that provide information and explanations about your code. They play a crucial role, especially when multiple people are working on the same set of code. Comments help with code analysis, leaving feedback, and even debugging.

There are two types of comments you can use in Python:

1. Single-line comment: These are short comments that occupy a single line. You can add them by using the '#' symbol before the comment text.

Program code:

```
# This is a single-line comment explaining the purpose of the following code
```

2. Multiple-line comment: Also known as a multiline comment, these are used when you need to write longer explanations that span across multiple lines. You can enclose multiline comments within triple quotes (''' ''').

Program code:

```
"""
This is a multiline comment, and it can be really helpful when you want to provide detailed explanations about your code.

You can use as many lines as needed to convey your message clearly.
"""
```

Adding comments is a great practice that not only helps you understand your code better but also aids other developers who might work with your code in the future.

18. What are global, protected, and private attributes in Python?

In Python, attributes of a class, which are also known as variables, can have different levels of accessibility. There are three main access modifiers for variables:

1. Public Attributes:

Public attributes are declared using regular variable names and can be accessed from anywhere, both inside and outside the class. They are widely accessible and provide easy access to data.

2. Private Attributes:

Private attributes are declared using a single underscore before the variable name (e.g., `**_variable**`). They are accessible only within the class where they are defined. This means that other classes or parts of the code cannot directly access these variables. Private attributes are useful when you want to restrict direct access to certain data and enforce encapsulation.

3. Protected Attributes:

Protected attributes are declared using a double underscore before the variable name (e.g., `**__variable**`). While they are not truly private like double-underscore variables in Python, they have a name-mangling mechanism, which makes them harder to access from outside the class. Protected attributes are accessible only within the current package and are typically used to indicate that a variable is intended for internal use within the class and its subclasses.

Attributes can also be classified based on their scope:

- **Local Attributes:** Local attributes are defined within a specific code block or method and can only be accessed within that particular block or method. They have a limited scope and are useful for temporary data storage within a specific context.

- **Global Attributes:** Global attributes are defined outside any code block or method and are accessible from anywhere in the program. They have a broader scope and can be used across different parts of the code.

Program code:

```
class Mobile:
    m1 = "Samsung Mobiles"  # Global attribute

    def price(self):
        m2 = "Costly mobiles"  # Local attribute
        return m2

Sam_m = Mobile()
print(Sam_m.m1)
```

Output:

```
"Samsung Mobiles"
```

In this example, `**m1**` is a global attribute accessible from outside the class, and `**m2**` is a local attribute accessible only within the `**price()**` method.

19. What are the different types of operators in Python?

Python offers a bunch of basic operators that allow you to perform various operations.

Let's take a quick look at them:

1. Arithmetic Operators: These are used for basic math operations like addition (+), subtraction (-), multiplication (*), division (/), and modulus (%), which gives you the remainder after division.

2. Relational Operators: These operators are handy for comparisons. You've got less than (<), greater than (>), less than or equal to (<=), greater than or equal to (>=), equal to (==), and not equal to (!=). They help you make decisions based on different conditions.

3. Assignment Operators: When you need to assign values to variables, you can use the assignment operators. The most common one is (=), but you also have +=, -=, *=, /=, and %=, which are shortcuts for performing operations and assigning the result back to the variable.

4. Logical Operators: With logical operators (and, or, not), you can combine conditions and create more complex expressions. They're essential for controlling the flow of your program based on multiple conditions.

5. Membership Operators: Python has (in and not in) operators to check if a value exists in a sequence (like a list, tuple, or string) or not. These come in handy when you need to search for specific elements.

6. Identity Operators: The identity operators (is and is not) help you compare the memory location of two objects. They come into play when you want to check if two variables refer to the same object or not.

7. Bitwise Operators: These operators perform operations at the bit level and are used in low-level programming. They include bitwise AND (&), OR (|), XOR (^), NOT (~), left shift (<<), and right shift (>>).

20. How to check the Python version in command prompt (CMD)

To find out which version of Python you have in Command Prompt, follow these simple steps:

Open Command Prompt:
Press the Windows key + Spacebar, and this will bring up the Spotlight search. In the search bar, type `**cmd**` and hit Enter. This opens the Command Prompt.

Check Python Version:
Once you're in the Command Prompt, simply type either of the following commands and hit Enter:

```
python --version
```

or

```
python -V
```

This will display the Python version on the next line.

Let's see it in action:

```
C:\Users\YourName> python --version
Python 3.9.2
```

This is how you can quickly check the Python version on your computer using the Command Prompt.

21. Is Python case sensitive when dealing with identifiers?

Absolutely! Python is indeed case-sensitive when it comes to identifiers. This means that Python treats uppercase and lowercase letters differently. For instance, in Python, a variable named `**variable**` and one named `**Variable**` are not the same thing

Program code:

```
variable = 10
Variable = 20
print(variable)
print(Variable)
```

Output:

```
10
20
```

In this example, we have two variables, one with a lowercase name and the other with an uppercase name. Python treats them as separate entities, and they can hold different values. So, remember to be consistent with your letter casing in Python!

22. How does Python manage memory?

In Python, memory management is handled automatically, which is great news for beginners. You don't need to worry about allocating or deallocating memory like in other languages. Python's memory manager takes care of this for you.

Useful tip:

- While Python's automatic memory management is convenient, it's still a good practice to manage your resources properly, especially when dealing with large datasets or long-running processes. Close files, release database connections, and clean up after yourself to help Python's memory management run even smoother.

What to remember:

- Python uses a concept called "garbage collection" to automatically reclaim memory occupied by objects no longer in use. You don't have to free up memory manually.
- Python manages memory efficiently to minimize your application's memory footprint.

23. What is the difference between .py and .pyc files?

In Python, you'll come across two file types:**.py** and **.pyc**. Let's break down the key differences between them to help you understand their roles:

.py Files (Source Code):

- These are your Python source code files.
- They contain the human-readable code that you write to create Python programs.

- **.py** files are what you work with when you're developing and writing Python scripts.

.pyc Files (Compiled Bytecode):

- **.pyc** files are compiled files generated by the Python compiler (usually created automatically).
- They store bytecode, which is a lower-level representation of your Python code.
- You don't typically need to create **.pyc** files manually; they are usually generated by Python when needed.
- **.pyc** files are mostly associated with Python's built-in modules and packages.

What to pay attention to:

- When you run your Python program, Python first compiles your **.py** files into **.pyc** files (if necessary) to improve execution speed. The **.pyc** files are stored in the `` `__pycache__` `` directory within your project folder.

Useful tip:

- If you're curious about how Python stores these compiled files, you can find **.pyc** files in the `` `__pycache__` `` directory. They have names that match the corresponding **.py** file's name.

What to remember:

- You typically won't interact with **.pyc** files directly during your regular Python development.

In summary, **.py** files contain your readable Python code, while **.pyc** files store the compiled bytecode. As a beginner, you won't need to create **.pyc** files manually; Python takes care of this process for you. Just focus on writing your Python code in **.py** files, and Python will handle the rest behind the scenes.

Python Data Types and Variables

24. How do you declare and use variables in Python?

Declaring and using variables in Python is a fundamental skill every beginner has. Here's a simple breakdown to get you started:

Declaration:
In Python, you don't need to declare the variable type explicitly. Just choose a name and assign a value using the equal sign (`=`). For example:

Program code:
```
my_variable = 42
name = "Python"
```

Usage:
Once you've declared a variable, you can use its value in various ways. For instance:

Program code:
```
result = my_variable * 2
greeting = "Hello, " + name
```

Let's say you want to calculate the area of a rectangle. You can use variables like this:

Program code:
```
length = 5
width = 3

area = length * width
print("The area of the rectangle is:", area)
```

Output:
```
The area of the rectangle is: 15
```

What to pay attention to:
- Variable names are case-sensitive, so `**my_variable**` and `**My_Variable**` are different.
- Choose descriptive names for better code readability.

Useful tips:
- Be consistent with naming conventions (e.g., use snake_case).
- Initialize variables before using them to avoid errors.

What to remember:
- No need to declare variable types.
- Use the equal sign (`=`) for assignment.
- Python is dynamic, allowing you to change a variable's value on the fly.

25. List the common built-in data types in Python?

Python offers a variety of built-in data types that we frequently use. Let's take a closer look at them:

1. Numbers: This data type encompasses integers, floating-point numbers, and complex numbers.

2. List: A list is an ordered sequence of items that can be changed or modified. It allows elements of different data types.

Program code:
```
my_list = [100, "Great Learning", 30]
```

3. Tuples: Similar to lists, tuples are also ordered sequences of elements. However, unlike lists, tuples are immutable, meaning they cannot be changed once defined.

Program code:
```
my_tuple = (100, "Great Learning", 20)
```

4. String: Strings are sequences of characters enclosed in either single or double quotes.

Program code:
```
my_string = "Hi, I work at Great Learning"
```

5. Sets: Sets are collections of unique items, and their order is not fixed.

Program code:
```
my_set = {1, 2, 3}
```

6. Dictionary: A dictionary stores values as key-value pairs, allowing easy access to each value using its associated key.

Program code:

```
my_dict = {1: 'video_games', 2: 'sports', 3: 'content'}
```

7. Boolean: Boolean data type has only two possible values, True and False, representing logical truth values.

Program code:

```
my_boolean = True
```

These are some of the fundamental data types in Python that you'll often encounter during interviews.

26. Explain the difference between mutable and immutable data types

Mutable data types, like lists, can be modified after creation.

For instance, consider a list: `**my_list = [1, 2, 3]**`. You can change its elements using indices: `**my_list[0] = 4**`, and now `**my_list**` is `**[4, 2, 3]**`.

Conversely, immutable data types, such as tuples, cannot be altered once created. If you have a tuple: `**my_tuple = (1, 2, 3)**`, trying to modify it like `**my_tuple[0] = 4**` will result in an error.

Here's a quick breakdown to keep in mind:

Mutable Data Types:

- Examples: Lists, Sets, Dictionaries (values, not keys)
- Can be modified after creation.
- Useful when you need dynamic data that can change.

Immutable Data Types:

- Examples: Tuples, Strings, Integers, Floats
- Cannot be changed after creation.
- Provide stability and security.

What to remember:

- When choosing a data type, consider whether you need the flexibility to modify its elements.
- Mutable types are handy for dynamic data, while immutable types provide consistency and safety.

Program code:

```
# Mutable Example (List)
my_list = [1, 2, 3]
my_list[0] = 4
print(my_list)
```

Output:

```
[4, 2, 3]
```

Program code:

```
# Immutable Example (Tuple)
my_tuple = (1, 2, 3)
# The line below would raise an error:
my_tuple[0] = 4
```

Output:

```
TypeError: 'tuple' object does not support item assignment
```

Understanding the mutability of data types is crucial for efficient and error-free Python programming.

27. What is variable scope in Python?

In Python, the accessibility of a variable is determined by its declaration location, which is known as the variable's scope. Scope resolution refers to the order in which Python looks for a variable's name when you use it. Let's explore the different scopes in Python and how scope resolution works:

Local Scope - Variables declared within a function or loop are accessible only within that specific function or loop.

Program code:

```
def my_function():
    local_variable = 42
    print(local_variable)

my_function()
print(local_variable) # This will result in an error, as 'local_variable' is not accessible outside the function.
```

Global Scope - Variables declared outside any function or loop at the topmost level of your code are accessible from anywhere in your program.

Program code:

```
global_variable = 100

def my_function():
    print(global_variable)

my_function()
print(global_variable) # You can access 'global_variable' from both inside and outside the function.
```

Enclosing Scope - Variables declared within an enclosing function are accessible only within that specific enclosing function.

Program code:

```
def outer_function():
    outer_variable = 5

    def inner_function():
        print(outer_variable)

    inner_function()

outer_function()
print(outer_variable) # This will result in an error because 'outer_variable' is not accessible outside its function.
```

Built-in Scope - Variables declared inside the built-in functions of various Python modules have built-in scope and are accessible only within their respective modules.

Program code:

```
import math

result = math.sqrt(25)
print(result)  # 'math' module's functions like 'sqrt' can be used, but
'result' is in the global scope.
```

Python performs scope resolution in a specific order:

Local Scope -> **Enclosing Scope** -> **Global Scope** -> **Built-in Scope**

Remember that when a variable is found in one of these scopes, Python stops searching for it. Understanding scope resolution is crucial when working with variables in Python, as it ensures you access the correct variable at the right time.

28. What is the difference between shallow and deep copying of data structures?

Understanding the distinction between shallow and deep copying in Python is crucial for effective data manipulation. Let's dive into it with practical examples to make it beginner-friendly.

Shallow copy

A shallow copy creates a new object but doesn't create copies of nested objects. Instead, it copies references to them. This means changes made to nested objects will reflect in both the original and copied data structures.

Program code:

```
import copy

original_list = [1, [2, 3], 4]
shallow_copy = copy.copy(original_list)
```

```
# Modify the nested list in the shallow copy
shallow_copy[1][0] = 99

print(original_list)
```

Output:

```
[1, [99, 3], 4]
```

What to pay attention to:

- Shallow copy is a quicker operation compared to deep copy.
- It's suitable when you don't want to replicate the entire object hierarchy.

Useful tip:

- A shallow copy might be sufficient if your data structure has only simple, non-nested objects.

What to remember:

- Changes to nested objects affect both the original and the shallow copy.

Deep copy

A deep copy creates a new object and recursively copies all objects found in the original. Changes made to nested objects in a deep copy won't affect the original data structure.

Program code:

```
import copy

original_list = [1, [2, 3], 4]
deep_copy = copy.deepcopy(original_list)

# Modify the nested list in the deep copy
deep_copy[1][0] = 99

print(original_list)
```

Output:

```
[1, [99, 3], 4]
```

What to pay attention to:

- Deep copy is a bit slower, especially for large and complex structures.
- It ensures complete independence between the original and copied data structures.

Useful tip:

- Opt for a deep copy when dealing with intricate data structures or when you need to maintain the independence of the copied structure.

What to remember:

- Changes to nested objects only affect the deep copy.

Understanding when to use shallow and deep copies can save you from unexpected behavior in your Python programs. Remember these distinctions, and choose the right copying method based on your specific use case.

Python File Operations and Handling

29. Explain the file processing modes that Python supports

In Python, when working with files, it's crucial to understand the different modes in which you can open them. These modes determine how you interact with the file, be it for reading, writing, or both.

Primary Modes:

`**r**` - Read-only mode. Opens the file for reading. (Default mode)

`**w**` - Write mode. Opens the file for writing. Creates a new file if it doesn't exist or truncates the file if it exists.

`**a**` - Append mode. Opens the file for writing, but data is appended at the end. If the file doesn't exist, it creates a new one.

`**b**` - Binary mode. Opens the file as binary rather than text. Useful for non-text files like images and sounds.

`**x**` - Exclusive creation mode. Opens the file for exclusive creation. If the file already exists, the operation will fail.

Combinations:

`**rb**`, `**wb**`, `**ab**`, `**xb**` - Combine read, write, append, or exclusive creation with binary mode.

- Reading a text file:

```
with open('sample.txt', 'r') as f:
    content = f.read()
```

- Writing to a text file:

```
with open('sample.txt', 'w') as f:
    f.write("Hello, Python!")
```

- Appending to a text file:

```
with open('sample.txt', 'a') as f:
    f.write("\nAppended text.")
```

- Reading a binary file (e.g., image):

```
with open('sample.jpg', 'rb') as f:
    data = f.read()
```

Useful tips:

- Always use the `**with**` statement when working with files in Python. It ensures that the file is properly closed after its suite finishes.
- Be cautious when using the `**w**` mode, as it can overwrite existing content.

What to remember:

- Python supports multiple file modes for various operations: read (`**r**`), write (`**w**`), append (`**a**`), binary (`**b**`), and exclusive creation (`**x**`).
- Combining modes, like `**rb**` or `**wb**`, can benefit specific tasks.
- The `with` statement provides a clean and efficient way to handle file operations.

30. How do you open and close files in Python?

In Python, mastering file handling is a fundamental skill. Let's dive into the essentials of opening and closing files, ensuring you navigate this crucial aspect with ease.

Opening files

To open a file, use the `**open()**` function. Specify the file name along with the mode, indicating whether you're reading ('**r**'), writing ('**w**'), or appending ('**a**'). Here's a simple example:

Program code:

```
# Opening a file in read mode
file_path = "example.txt"
with open(file_path, 'r') as file:
    content = file.read()
    print(content)
```

Closing files

While the `**with**` statement takes care of closing files, understanding how to manually close is crucial. Consider this example:

Program code:

```
file_path = "example.txt"
file = open(file_path, 'r')
content = file.read()
print(content)
file.close()
```

What to pay attention to:

- If you forget to close a file, it may lead to unexpected behavior or issues with resource management.
- Prioritize the `` `with` `` statement for cleaner and safer code.

Useful tips:

- Explore different modes like '**w**' for writing and '**a**' for appending to suit your needs.
- Leverage the `` `read()` ``, `` `readline()` ``, or `` `readlines()` `` methods based on your reading requirements.

What to remember:

- Always use the `` `with` `` statement when opening files. It ensures proper handling and automatically closes the file when done.
- Check the file path and ensure it's correct.

31. How do you delete a file in Python?

To delete a file, you'll need to use the `` `os` `` module, which is a part of the Python standard library. Specifically, we'll use the `` `os.remove()` `` function.

Program code:

```
import os

# Specify the file you want to delete
file_path = "example.txt"

# Check if the file exists before deleting
if os.path.exists(file_path):
    os.remove(file_path)
    print(f"{file_path} has been deleted.")
else:
    print(f"{file_path} does not exist.")
```

What to pay attention to:

- Make sure you provide the correct file path to `**os.remove()**`.
- Always check if the file exists before attempting to delete it to avoid errors.

Useful tip:

- If you need to work with directories (folders) rather than files, you can use `**os.rmdir()**` to remove an empty directory or `**shutil.rmtree()**` to remove a directory and its contents.

What to remember:

- Deleting a file is a permanent action, and it cannot be undone. Be cautious when using this operation.

32. What is the `with` statement in Python?

The `**with**` statement in Python is a nifty tool for handling exceptions and managing files more efficiently. When you have a block of code that needs to work with a file, you can use the `**with**` statement to open and close the file automatically, without the need for explicitly calling the `**close()**` function.

So, why is this important? Well, using the `**with**` statement not only helps you avoid potential bugs by ensuring the file is properly closed after use, but it also makes your code much more readable and concise. No more worrying about forgetting to close the file and dealing with unnecessary complications!

Here's an example of using the `**with**` statement for file handling in Python:

Suppose we have a text file named "example.txt" with the following content:

example.txt:

```
Hello, this is an example file.
We are using the 'with statement' in Python.
It makes file handling much easier!
```

Now, let's read the contents of this file using the `**with**` statement:

Program code:

```
# Using 'with statement' to read a file
file_path = 'example.txt'

try:
    with open(file_path, 'r') as file:
        content = file.read()
        print(content)
except FileNotFoundError:
    print(f"The file '{file_path}' was not found.")
```

When you run this code, it will open the "example.txt" file, read its content, and then print it to the console:

Output:

```
Hello, this is an example file.
We are using the 'with statement' in Python.
It makes file handling much easier!
```

Notice that we didn't explicitly close the file using `**file.close()**`; the `**with**` statement automatically takes care of that for us. It ensures that the file is closed properly after the block of code (inside the `**with**` block) is executed or if an exception occurs.

Using the `**with**` statement simplifies the process of file handling and improves the readability of the code. It's a recommended practice when dealing with files in Python.

In a nutshell, the `**with**` statement simplifies file handling in Python and promotes cleaner, more elegant code. It's definitely something you'll encounter often in Python development and a handy concept to be familiar with during interviews!

33. How do you read and write text files in Python?

Python makes handling text files a breeze. Whether you're reading data or storing information, understanding file operations is essential.

Reading text files

To read a file, use the `**open()**` function:

Program code:

```
# Open a file in read mode
with open('example.txt', 'r') as file:
    content = file.read()
    print(content)
```

Useful tip:

- If you're dealing with large files, consider reading line by line using a loop or `**readline()**` for efficiency.

What to remember:

- The `**'r'**` mode stands for read.
- Always use `**with open()**` to ensure the file is properly closed after reading.

Writing text files

To write to a file, open it in write mode (`**'w'**`):

Program code:

```
# Open a file in write mode
with open('output.txt', 'w') as file:
    file.write('Hello, Python!')
```

Useful tip:

- To append content without overwriting, use `**'a'**` mode instead of `**'w'**`.

What to remember:

- The `**'w'**` mode creates a new file or truncates an existing one.
- Be cautious, as writing in this mode will overwrite the file's existing content.

Handling exceptions

Always be prepared for potential errors when working with files:

Program code:

```
try:
    with open('nonexistent_file.txt', 'r') as file:
        content = file.read()
        print(content)
except FileNotFoundError:
    print('File not found! Check the file path.')
```

What to remember:

- Handle exceptions to prevent crashes when dealing with files.

Key takeaways:

1. Use `**with open()**` for proper file handling.
2. Pay attention to file modes (`**'r'**`, `**'w'**`, `**'a'**`).
3. Be cautious when writing to avoid unintentional data loss.

34. Describe binary file handling in Python.

In Python, handling binary files allows us to work with data in its raw, binary form. Unlike text files, binary files store information in a format that's not human-readable but is highly efficient for machines.

Creating a binary File

To embark on our journey, let's create a binary file. Imagine we want to store the bytes representing a colorful image.

Program code:

```
# Opening a binary file in write mode
with open("colorful_image.bin", "wb") as file:
    # Example byte data (replace with your actual binary data)
    byte_data = b'\x12\x34\x56\x78\x9a\bc\xde\xf0'

    # Writing the byte data to the file
    file.write(byte_data)
```

Useful tip:

- The `**"wb"**` mode stands for "write binary". It ensures that the file is treated as a binary file.

Reading from a binary File

Now, let's retrieve our precious binary data from the file.

Program code:

```
# Opening the binary file in read mode
with open("colorful_image.bin", "rb") as file:
    # Reading the entire content of the file
    binary_data = file.read()

    # Displaying the binary data
    print(f"Binary Data: {binary_data}")
```

What to pay attention to:

- Always use the `**"rb"**` mode when reading from a binary file to avoid encoding issues.

Useful tip:

- For more advanced binary file handling, check out Python's `**struct**` module. It helps you pack and unpack binary data into and from Python data types.

Program code:

```
import struct

# Example: Packing integers into binary data
binary_data = struct.pack("II", 42, 99)
print(f"Packed Data: {binary_data}")
```

What to remember:

- Binary files don't have newline characters or text encoding. You're dealing with the raw essence of data, so handle it with care.
- The format string in `**struct.pack**` specifies the data types and their order.

35. How to save images locally with Python?

Saving images locally with Python is a common task, and the go-to method involves using the `**open()**` function in conjunction with the binary write mode (`**'wb'**`). This process entails reading image data from a source and then writing it to a new file.

To facilitate fetching image data, the requests library proves to be invaluable. If you haven't installed it yet, a quick `**pip install requests**` will do the trick.

Program code:

```
import requests

def save_image_from_url(url, filename):
    response = requests.get(url)
    if response.status_code == 200:
        with open(filename, 'wb') as file:
            file.write(response.content)
        print(f"Image saved as {filename}")
    else:
        print("Failed to download the image")

# Replace these values with your image URL and desired file name
image_url = "https://example.com/image.jpg"
output_filename = "saved_image.jpg"

# Save the image
save_image_from_url(image_url, output_filename)
```

36. What is pickling and unpickling?

`**Pickling**` is a term used in Python to describe the process of converting a Python object into a byte stream. This byte stream can be stored in a file, sent over a network, or even stored in a database. On the flip side, `**unpickling**` is the process of converting that byte stream back into its original Python object.

Pickling an object

Program code:

```
import pickle

data = {"name": "John", "age": 30, "city": "New York"}
# Pickling the data dictionary
with open("data.pkl", "wb") as file:
    pickle.dump(data, file)
```

This code takes a dictionary `**data**` and `**pickles**` it into a file named `**data.pkl**`.

Unpickling an object

Program code:

```
import pickle

# Unpickling the data
with open("data.pkl", "rb") as file:
   loaded_data = pickle.load(file)
print(loaded_data) # Output: {'name': 'John', 'age': 30, 'city': 'New York'}
```

Here, the data is `**unpickled**` from the `**data.pkl**` file and then printed.

Useful tips:

- **Be Cautious**: Don't unpickle data from untrusted or unknown sources. Malicious data can execute arbitrary code during unpickling.
- **File Modes**: Always use binary mode (`**wb**` for writing and `**rb**` for reading) when pickling and unpickling.

What to remember:

- Pickling transforms Python objects into byte streams.
- Unpickling does the reverse, converting byte streams back into Python objects.
- It's a handy way to serialize and deserialize data, but always be cautious with data sources.

Control Flow

37. Describe Python's conditional statements (if, elif, else).

Conditional statements in Python - such as `**if**`, `**elif**`, and `**else**` - are powerful tools that allow your code to make decisions based on certain conditions. They help your program respond dynamically to different situations.

- `**if**` **statement**: Use this when executing a block of code only if a certain condition is true.

Program code:

```
if condition:
    # code to execute if the condition is true
```

- `**elif**` **statement:** Short for "**else if**," this allows you to check multiple conditions if the previous ones are false.

```
Program code:
if condition1:
    # code to execute if condition1 is true
elif condition2:
    # code to execute if condition2 is true
```

- `**else**` **statement:** This is used to execute a code block if none of the preceding conditions are true.

Program code:

```
if condition:
    # code to execute if the condition is true
else:
    # code to execute if the condition is false
```

Let's consider a scenario where we want to determine if a number is positive, negative, or zero.

Program code:

```
num = 10

if num > 0:
    print("The number is positive")
elif num < 0:
    print("The number is negative")
else:
    print("The number is zero")
```

What to pay attention to:

- **Indentation matters:** Python uses indentation to define code blocks. Make sure to maintain consistent indentation for proper execution.
- **Conditions should be boolean:** Ensure that the conditions in your `**if**`, `**elif**`, and `**else**` statements evaluate to either `**True**` or `**False**`.

Useful tips:

- **Combine conditions:** You can use logical operators (`**and**`, `**or**`, `**not**`) to create more complex conditions.
- **Nested statements:** You can nest conditional statements within each other for more intricate decision-making.

What to remember:

- **Order of evaluation:** Conditions are evaluated from top to bottom. Once a true condition is found, the associated block of code is executed, and the rest are skipped.
- **Default execution:** If no `**elif**` or `**else**` condition is met, the default behavior is to execute the `else` block or simply move on if there is none.

38. Explain the concept of loops in Python (for, while)

In Python, loops are your secret weapon for handling repetitive tasks. Let's dive into two essential types: the `**for**` loop and the `**while**` loop.

The `for` loop

A `**for**` loop is your go-to when you know in advance how many times you want to repeat a block of code. It's like having a superpower for handling lists, strings, or any iterable object.

Program code:
```
fruits = ["apple", "banana", "cherry"]

for fruit in fruits:
    print(fruit)
```

What to pay attention to:

- The colon at the end of the `**for**` statement signals the start of the loop.
- Proper indentation is crucial. Python uses it to understand which code is part of the loop.

Useful tip:

- The `**range()**` function is an excellent ally in creating numerical sequences for your `**for**` loops.

The `while` loop

When unsure how often you must repeat a code block, the `**while**` loop comes to the rescue. It keeps looping until a specified condition becomes False.

Program code:
```
count = 0

while count < 5:
    print("Count is:", count)
    count += 1
```

Useful tip:

- `**while**` loops are fantastic for scenarios where you're waiting for a specific user input or event.

What to remember:

- Ensure the loop's condition eventually becomes False to prevent an infinite loop.
- Increment or decrement the loop control variable inside the loop to avoid endless repetition.

Loops are your trusty companions in Python programming. Whether you're iterating through a list or executing a block of code until a condition is met, mastering loops unlocks the true potential of your Python skills.

39. Briefly explain about `break`, `pass` and `continue` statements in Python?

In Python, we have three handy control flow statements that help us manage loops and conditional structures effectively: `**break**`, `**pass**`, and `**continue**`. Let's explore their roles and usage:

Break statement

What it does:

When you use a `**break**` statement in your Python code or program, it immediately terminates the current loop and transfers control to the statement following the loop.

What to pay attention to:

`**break**` is often used to exit a loop prematurely when a specific condition is met, saving time and resources.

Program code:

```
numbers = [10, 20, 30, 40, 50]
for num in numbers:
    if num == 30:
        break
    print(num)
```

Output:

```
10, 20
```

Continue statement

What it does:

The `**continue**` statement in Python is used to break out of the current iteration of a loop. It skips the rest of the code within the current iteration and proceeds to the next iteration of the loop.

What to pay attention to:

`**continue**` is handy when you want to skip specific items in a loop or perform different actions based on conditions.

Program code:

```
numbers = [1, 2, 3, 4, 5]
for num in numbers:
    if num % 2 == 0:
        continue
    print(num)
```

Output:

```
1, 3, 5
```

Pass statement

What it does:

When executed, the `pass` statement in Python serves as a placeholder or a **Null** operation. While the interpreter doesn't overlook this statement, it essentially results in no action being taken. It comes into play when you need a syntactical element but you don't want any specific command or action to be executed at that point. This can be particularly useful when structuring your code and must include a statement for future implementation without triggering any immediate functionality.

What to pay attention to:

- It's like a temporary `**no-op**` operation, allowing you to create the skeleton of your code without immediate functionality.

Program code:

```
GL = [10, 30, 20, 100, 212, 33, 13, 50, 60, 70]
for g in GL:
    pass
    if g == 0:
        current = g
        break
    elif g % 2 == 0:
        continue
    print(g)
```

Output:

```
33
13
```

What to remember:

- Using these statements effectively can enhance your Python coding skills and make your code more efficient. `**break**`, `**pass**`, and `**continue**` are valuable tools in your Python programming toolbox.

40. What is the difference between xrange and range in Python?

In Python, you'll often encounter the need to generate a sequence of integer numbers within a specified range. This is where the `**range()**` and `**xrange()**` functions come into play. However, there's a significant difference between these two in Python 2.0, which is important to understand. In Python 3.0 and beyond, `**xrange()**` is re-implemented as `**range()**`, so the difference no longer applies.

Here's what you need to know in Python 2.

1. Memory usage:
- `**range()**` consumes more memory compared to `**xrange()**`.

2. Execution speed:
- `**xrange()**` is faster in terms of execution speed compared to `**range()**`.

3. Return types:
- `**range()**` returns a list of integers, whereas `**xrange()**` returns a generator object.

Program code:

```
# Using range()
for i in range(1, 10, 2):
    print(i)
```

This code will output the numbers 1, 3, 5, 7, and 9, as the `**range()**` function generates a list of integers.

What to remember:

- If you're using Python 3.0 or newer, there's no need to worry about the differences between `**range()**` and `**xrange()**`, as they are functionally equivalent.
- In Python 2.0, if you want to save memory or improve performance when dealing with large ranges, consider using `**xrange()**`. However, for most cases, `**range()**` will serve you well.

41. How to determine if a number is even or odd in Python?

In Python, you can easily create a function to check if a number is even or odd. Here's a simple function to do just that:

Program code:

```
def even_odd(x):
    if x % 2 == 0:
        print(x, " is even")
    else:
        print(x, " is odd")
```

Code explanation:

- We define a function called `**even_odd**` that takes one parameter, `**x**`.
- Inside the function, we use the modulo operator (%) to check if `**x**` is divisible by 2. If the remainder is 0, it's even; otherwise, it's odd.
- We print the result with a clear message indicating whether the number is even or odd.

Now, let's put it into action:

Program code:

```
even_odd(5)
```

When we call `**even_odd(5)**`, the function will print:

Output:

```
5 is odd
```

It tells us that the number 5 is indeed odd. You can use this function to check evenness or oddness for any integer you need. It's a handy tool for simple number analysis in Python!

42. Calculate the factorial of a number in Python

The factorial calculation is a classic problem in Python interviews. Let's write a Python program to calculate the factorial of a number.

Here's how to do it:

Program code:

```
# Take input from the user
num = int(input("Enter a number: "))

# Initialize the factorial to 1
factorial = 1

# Check if the number is negative, zero, or positive
if num < 0:
   print("Sorry, factorial does not exist for negative numbers")
elif num == 0:
   print("The factorial of 0 is 1")
else:
   # Calculate the factorial for positive numbers
   for i in range(1, num + 1):
      factorial *= i
   print("The factorial of", num, "is", factorial)
```

What to pay attention to:

- We take user input for the number they want to find the factorial of.
- We handle negative numbers and zero separately, as factorial is not defined for negative numbers, and the factorial of 0 is 1.
- For positive numbers, we use a for loop to calculate the factorial.
- We use the `**factorial**` variable to keep track of the result, which starts at 1 and gets updated in each iteration.

Useful tip:

- Factorial is an excellent example to practice using loops in Python.

43. Check if a number is a palindrome

You want to determine whether a given number is a palindrome or not. A palindrome is a number that reads the same backward as forward, like 121 or 1331.

To check if a number is a palindrome, follow this Python program:

Program code:

```
n = int(input("Enter a number:")) # Input the number
temp = n  # Make a copy of the original number
rev = 0  # Initialize a variable to store the reversed number

while n > 0:  # Start a loop that runs until n becomes 0
    dig = n % 10  # Get the last digit of n
    rev = rev * 10 + dig  # Reverse the number by adding the last digit
    n = n // 10  # Remove the last digit from n

if temp == rev:  # Compare the reversed number with the original number
    print("The number is a palindrome!")
else:
    print("The number isn't a palindrome!")
```

Code explanation:

- We start by taking an input number and storing it in the variable `**n**`.
- We make a copy of the original number in the variable `**temp**`.
- Initialize a variable `**rev**` to 0. This variable will store the reversed number.
- Enter a `**while**` loop that continues until `**n**` becomes 0.
- Inside the loop, we get the last digit of `**n**` using the modulo operator `**%**` and store it in the variable `**dig**`.
- We reverse the number by multiplying `**rev**` by 10 and adding `**dig**` to it. This result is stored back in `**rev**`.
- We remove the last digit from `**n**` by performing integer division `**n // 10**`.
- After the loop ends, we compare the values of `**rev**` and `**temp**`. If they are equal, we print "**The number is a palindrome**". Otherwise, we print "**The number isn't a palindrome**".

Useful tips:

- Remember that a palindrome is a number that reads the same forwards and backward.
- Make use of variables to keep track of the original number and the reversed number.
- Be careful with the order of operations in reversing the number.

Now you can easily check whether a number is a palindrome or not

44. How can you print the 2-times table using a while loop in Python?

To create a program that prints the 2-times table using a while loop, follow this code:

Program code:

```
i = 1
n = 2

while i <= 10:
    result = n * i
    print(f"{n} * {i} = {result}")
    i += 1
```

Output:

```
2 * 1 = 2
2 * 2 = 4
2 * 3 = 6
2 * 4 = 8
2 * 5 = 10
2 * 6 = 12
2 * 7 = 14
2 * 8 = 16
2 * 9 = 18
2 * 10 = 20
```

Code explanation:

- We start by initializing two variables, `**i**` and `**n**`. `**i**` is set to 1, and `**n**` is set to 2.
- Inside the while loop, the `**i**` value starts at 1 and goes up to 10. This loop will iterate 10 times.
- We calculate the result of `**n * i**` and store it in the `**result**` variable.
- Then, we use the `**print**` statement to display the result in the format `**n * i = result**`.
- After each iteration, we increment the `**i**` value by 1 using `**i += 1**`, so it progresses from 1 to 2, 3, and so on, up to 10.
- This process continues until the `**i**` value reaches 10, and the 2-times table is printed for each value of `**i**`.

Following this code, you can easily print the 2-times table in Python using a while loop. It's a simple and effective way to practice loops and multiplication in Python.

Python String

45. How to convert a string into lowercase?

In Python, you can easily convert all uppercase characters in a string to lowercase by using the method: `**string.lower()**`. Let me show you an example:

Program code:

```
string = 'HELLO WORLD'
print(string.lower())
```

Output:

```
hello world
```

By calling `**string.lower()**`, Python will automatically convert all the uppercase letters in the string to their lowercase equivalents, making it simple to work with different cases in your code.

46. How can you capitalize the first letter of a string?

To capitalize the first letter of a string in Python, you can use the `**capitalize()**` function. It's a handy method that does the job effortlessly. If the first character of the string is already capitalized, the function will return the original string as it is.

Syntax:

```
string_name.capitalize()
```

Program code:

```
text = "hellO World"
print(text.capitalize())
```

Output:

```
Hello world
```

Using the `**capitalize()**` function on the string "hellO World" results in "Helloworld" as the first letter gets capitalized. This method is useful when you want to standardize the capitalization of names, titles, or any strings that should begin with a capital letter.

47. Converting numbers to strings

When it comes to converting a number into a string in Python, the process is quite straightforward. Python offers a built-in function called `**str()**` that serves this purpose efficiently.

In Python, the `**str()**` function performs the conversion seamlessly. It takes a numeric value as its input and returns the equivalent string representation of that number. This functionality proves to be particularly useful when you're dealing with situations where you need to combine numbers with strings or display numeric values alongside text.

For instance, let's say you have a numerical value, and you want to include it in a sentence to create a meaningful output. By utilizing the `**str()**` function, you can effortlessly convert the number to a string and then concatenate it with other textual content.

Program code:

```
num = 42
text = "The lucky number is: " + str(num)
print(text)
```

In this snippet, the `**str()**` function converts the numeric value `**42**` into the string `**"42"**`, enabling it to be concatenated with the rest of the sentence.

Output:

```
The lucky number is: 42
```

So, whenever you encounter the need to transform a number into a string in Python, remember that the `**str()**` function is your go-to tool for achieving this task effectively.

48. How to reverse a string in Python?

To reverse a string in Python, you don't need any fancy tools. It's actually quite straightforward. We'll use an array slicing operation, which might sound intimidating, but it's simpler than it sounds.

Program code:

```
str_reverse = string[::-1]
```

Code explanation:

- We start with the string you want to reverse, let's call it `**string**`.

- We use slicing, which is denoted by the `**[::-1]**` part.
- The `**[::-1]**` slice tells Python to go through the string from the end to the beginning, effectively reversing it.

Example: Let's say you have the string "hello". If you apply this code:

Program code:

```
string = "hello"
str_reverse = string[::-1]
print(str_reverse)
```

Output:

```
"olleh"
```

That's it! You've successfully reversed a string in Python. It's a handy trick to know, especially when dealing with text manipulation tasks.

49. Removing spaces from a string

Sometimes, you might want to remove any spaces when working with strings in Python. This could be for formatting, comparison, or other reasons. Let's dive into how you can achieve this.

Program code:

```
s = "Hello, World! How are you?"
```

Now, if you want to remove all spaces, you'd do:

Program code:

```
no_spaces = s.replace(" ", "")
print(no_spaces)
```

Output:

```
Hello,World!Howareyou?
```

Useful tips:

- The `**replace()**` method is versatile. You can replace any character or set of characters in a string, not just spaces.
- Be careful when removing spaces as it might change the meaning or readability of your text.
- Use the `**replace()**` method to remove spaces from a string.

Python Lists, Tuples and Dictionaries

50. What is the difference between lists and tuples in Python?

Lists and tuples are two types of data structures in Python that allow you to store multiple objects or values in a single variable.

Let's take a closer look at their characteristics:

Lists:

- Lists are mutable, which means you can modify their elements after they are created. You can add or remove items from a list easily.
- However, due to their mutable nature, iterations and modifications in lists can be time-consuming in certain situations.
- Lists are more convenient when you need to perform actions like insertion and deletion of elements.
- They take up more memory compared to tuples, which is something to keep in mind when dealing with large datasets.
- Python provides numerous built-in methods that make working with lists very versatile.
- Since lists are mutable, there is a chance of unexpected changes or errors occurring during the program execution.

Tuples:

- Tuples, on the other hand, are immutable, meaning once they are created, you cannot change or modify their elements. They remain fixed.
- Iterations on tuples are generally faster compared to lists due to their immutability.
- Accessing items in a tuple is done using the tuple data type.
- Tuples consume less memory than lists, making them a good choice for situations where data should not be modified.
- Unlike lists, tuples have fewer built-in methods available.
- Because tuples are immutable, they offer more reliability and prevent accidental changes in critical data.

Creating a list:

```
my_list = [100, " Creating a list ", 30]
```

Creating a tuple:

```
my_tuple = (100, " Creating a tuple ", 20)
```

In summary, if you need a collection that can be modified or updated, you may choose a list. However, if you want to ensure data integrity and avoid unintended changes, a tuple would be the better option. Both lists and tuples have their strengths and use cases, so it's essential to choose the appropriate data structure based on the specific requirements of your program.

51. What is the difference between a tuple and a dictionary?

Well, the key difference lies in their mutability. A dictionary is like a magical box that can change its content without losing its identity. You can add, remove, or modify elements in a dictionary as much as you want, and it'll still be the same dictionary!

On the other hand, a tuple is more like a reliable, unchangeable container. Once you create a tuple, it's set in stone. You can't modify its elements or add new ones. It's all about consistency and keeping things safe.

So, in a nutshell: dictionaries are flexible and mutable, while tuples are steadfast and immutable.

52. What is the difference between arrays and lists in Python?

Both Python Arrays and Lists are handy tools for storing collections of elements, and they share common characteristics like being ordered and mutable. However, there are some important distinctions you should be aware of when deciding which one to use. Let's break it down:

Arrays:

- Arrays are part of the Python's `**array**` module and are primarily used to store homogeneous data. In other words, elements of an array should be of the same data type.
- You need to import the `**array**` module to use arrays effectively.
- Here's an example of creating an array and printing it:

Program code:

```
import array as a1
array1 = a1.array('i', [1, 2, 5])
print(array1)
```

or

Program code:

```
import numpy as a2
array2 = a2.array([5, 6, 9, 2])
print(array2)
```

Lists:

- Lists are more versatile as they can store heterogeneous data, meaning elements can have different data types within the same list.
- Lists are readily available in Python, and you don't need to import any specific module to use them.
- You can create a list and start using it without prior declaration.

Useful tip:

- If you're dealing with numerical data, especially when using mathematical operations, consider using arrays. They provide a more streamlined approach and better performance for such tasks.

What to remember:

- Arrays are specialized for storing homogeneous data types, while lists can handle a mix of data types.
- When working with numerical operations, arrays are often more convenient and efficient.

You can choose between arrays and lists depending on your specific needs. Arrays are ideal for homogeneous data, while lists offer greater flexibility when dealing with a variety of data types. Make the choice that best suits your project requirements and coding style.

53. How can you concatenate two tuples in Python?

Concatenating two tuples in Python means combining the elements of one tuple with the elements of another tuple. It's like putting them together to create a new tuple.

Imagine we have two tuples:

```
tup1 = (1, "a", True)
tup2 = (4, 5, 6)
```

To concatenate `**tup2**` with `**tup1**`, you can use the `**+**` operator like this:

Program code:

```
result = tup1 + tup2
```

The `**result**` will be a new tuple with elements from both `**tup1**` and `**tup2**` in that order.

Similarly, if you want to concatenate `**tup1**` with `**tup2**`, you just need to switch the order of operands:

Program code:

```
result = tup2 + tup1
```

With the `**+**` operator, you can easily concatenate two tuples in Python. It's a simple and effective way to combine the elements and create a new tuple.

54. What is a dictionary in Python?

A Python dictionary is a super useful collection that allows you to store items without any specific order. Imagine it like a magical bag that holds pairs of keys and values! You create dictionaries using curly brackets { } and separate each key-value pair with a colon (:).

Program code:

```
my_dictionary = {"a": 1, "b": 2}
```

In this example, we've created a dictionary called `**my_dictionary**`, which contains two key-value pairs: `**a**` with a value of 1, and `**b**` with a value of 2. The keys can be any immutable data type, like strings or numbers, and the values can be any data type, including numbers, strings, lists, or even other dictionaries!

One of the best things about dictionaries is that they're lightning-fast when it comes to retrieving values based on their keys. So, whenever you need to find a specific value, Python will take care of it in no time!

Dictionaries are super handy for tasks like storing settings, mapping relationships between different items, or counting occurrences of elements.

55. How do you get a list of all the keys in a dictionary?

Getting a list of keys from a dictionary is easy in Python! You can use the method `**dict.keys()**` to achieve this. When you call `**dict.keys()**`, it will return all the keys available in the dictionary.

For example, let's say we have the following dictionary:

```
my_dict = {1: 'a', 2: 'b', 3: 'c'}
```

To get a list of keys from this dictionary, you simply use `**my_dict.keys()**`, like this:

```
keys_list = my_dict.keys()
```

Output:

```
[1, 2, 3]
```

Now, `**keys_list**` contains all the keys present in the `**my_dict**` dictionary, which are `**[1, 2, 3]**`. This method is quite handy when you want to access or manipulate the keys separately from the values in the dictionary.

56. How can you insert an element at a given index in Python?

Python has got handy `**insert()**` function.

To insert an element at a particular index, you can simply use the `**insert()**` function with the following syntax:

Syntax:

```
list_name.insert(index, element)
```

Program code:

```
my_list = [0, 1, 2, 3, 4, 5, 6, 7]
# Let's insert 10 at the 6th index
my_list.insert(6, 10)
```

Output:

```
[0, 1, 2, 3, 4, 5, 10, 6, 7]
```

And there you have it! You've successfully inserted the element `**10**` at the 6th index in your list. The `**insert()**` function is a nifty way to modify your lists in Python and tailor them to your specific needs.

57. How will you remove duplicate elements from a list?

Removing duplicate elements from a list is a common task in Python, and there are various methods to achieve this. One of the most straightforward approaches is by using the set() function.

Here's a step-by-step guide on how to do it:

STEP 1: Identify the list with duplicate elements.

For example, let's consider the list named `**list0**`:

Program code:

```
list0 = [2, 6, 4, 7, 4, 6, 7, 2]
```

STEP 2: Convert the list into a set using the `**set()**` function. A set is an unordered collection of unique elements, so any duplicates in the original list will be automatically removed.

Program code:

```
unique_set = set(list0)
```

STEP 3: (Optional) If you need the result back as a list, convert the set back to a list using the `**list()**` function.

Program code:

```
list_without_duplicates = list(unique_set)
```

Here's the complete code to remove duplicates from the list `**list0**`:

Program code:

```
list0 = [2, 6, 4, 7, 4, 6, 7, 2]
unique_set = set(list0)
list_without_duplicates = list(unique_set)
print("The list without duplicates: " + str(list_without_duplicates))
```

Output:

```
The list without duplicates: [2, 4, 6, 7]
```

By following these simple steps, you can easily remove duplicate elements from a list in Python. This method is efficient and works well with lists of any size.

58. Explain Python list comprehension

Python List Comprehension is a nifty way to create a new list by transforming elements from an existing list. It's like a shortcut that lets you filter and modify data in a single line of code!

Here's how it works:

- You start with an expression that defines how you want each element to be in the new list.
- Then comes the "for" clause, where you specify the source list and a variable (let's call it "i") that represents each element in that list.
- Finally, everything is enclosed in square brackets to create the new list.

Program code:

```
# Suppose we want to create a list containing numbers from 0 to 999.
original_list = [i for i in range(1000)]

# Now, when we print the new list, it will look like this:
print(original_list)
```

Running this code will give you a list of numbers from 0 to 999.

The real magic of list comprehensions happens when you add conditions and transformations to the mix. You can do things like filtering elements based on specific criteria or even perform calculations on each element while creating the new list.

List comprehensions not only make your code shorter and more concise but also enhance its readability and maintainability.

59. How to find the minimum and maximum values in a tuple?

To find the minimum value in a tuple, you can use the `**min()**` function. Here's how it works:

Program code:

```
tup1 = (1, 2, 3, 4, 5)
minimum_value = min(tup1)
print(minimum_value)
```

Output:

```
1
```

In this example, the minimum value present in the tuple is 1.

Similarly, you can use the `**max()**` function to find the maximum value in a tuple:

Program code:

```
tup1 = (1, 2, 3, 4, 5)
maximum_value = max(tup1)
print(maximum_value)
```

Output:

```
5
```

Here, we find that the maximum value in the tuple is 5.

What to remember:

- To use these functions to quickly determine the minimum and maximum values in your tuples.

60. How to access specific elements in a mixed list?

In this scenario, you have a list containing a mix of different data types: [1, "a", 2, "b", 3, "c"]. Your task is to access the 2nd, 4th, and 5th elements from this list.

To accomplish this, we'll create a tuple that holds the indices of the elements we want to access. Then, we'll use a for loop to iterate through these index values and print out the corresponding elements. Here's the code to do it:

Program code:

```
my_list = [1, "a", 2, "b", 3, "c"]
indices_to_access = (1, 3, 4)

for index in indices_to_access:
    print(my_list[index])
```

Output:

```
a
b
3
```

What to pay attention to:

- Lists in Python are zero-indexed, meaning the first element is at index 0, the second at index 1, and so on.
- Ensure that the indices you specify are within the bounds of the list to avoid IndexError.

Useful tips:

- This method allows you to access specific elements from a list, regardless of their data types.
- You can customize the `**indices_to_access**` tuple to retrieve any elements you need from the list.

By following this approach, you can easily extract the desired elements from a mixed list in Python.

61. How to flip elements in the List?

In Python, reversing a list is a handy skill to have. Let's say you have a list like this one: ["sparta", True, 3+4j, False]. To flip its elements, we can use the `**reverse()**` function.

Here's how:

Program code:

```
a = ["sparta", True, 3+4j, False]
a.reverse()
print(a)
```

That's it! Now, you'll see the elements in reverse order

Output:

```
[False, (3+4j), True, 'sparta']
```

What to remember:

- To use the `**reverse()**` function directly on your list. It's a simple way to change the order of elements without creating a new list.

62. How can you update the value in a dictionary?

If you have a dictionary like this: `**fruit = {"Apple": 10, "Orange": 20, "Banana": 30, "Guava": 40}**`, how can you update the value of `**Apple**` from 10 to 100?

To update the value of `Apple`, you can simply follow these steps:

1. Identify the key you want to update, in this case, it's `**Apple**`.
2. Assign the new value to it, which is 100.

Here's the code to achieve this:

Program code:

```
fruit["Apple"] = 100
```

Now, when you check the `**fruit**` dictionary, you'll see that the value for `**Apple**` has been updated to 100.

63. How can you find the common elements in two sets?

You have two sets: `**s1 = {1,2,3,4,5,6}**` and `**s2 = {5,6,7,8,9}**`.

To find the common elements between these two sets, you can use the `**intersection()**` function.

Here's how you can do it:

Program code:

```
s1 = {1,2,3,4,5,6}
s2 = {5,6,7,8,9}
common_elements = s1.intersection(s2)
```

In this case, the common elements between the two sets are 5 and 6.

Useful tips:

- Remember that sets are a great way to store unique elements.
- The `**intersection()**` function is a handy tool for finding common elements between sets.
- Make sure to assign the result to a variable, like `**common_elements**`, so you can use it later in your code.

By using sets and the `**intersection()**` function, you can easily identify the shared elements between two sets, which is especially useful for tasks like data analysis and filtering.

64. Incrementing dictionary values

Imagine you have a dictionary like this:

Program code:

```
d1 = {"k1": 10, "k2": 20, "k3": 30}
```

How would you increment the values of all the keys in this dictionary?

To increment the values of all keys in the dictionary, you can use a for loop to iterate through the keys and update their values. Here's a simple code snippet to do that:

Program code:

```
d1 = {"k1": 10, "k2": 20, "k3": 30}

# Iterate through the keys and increment their values
for key in d1.keys():
    d1[key] += 1
```

What to pay attention to:

- Make sure you access the keys with `**d1.keys()**` or directly with a `**for key in d1**` loop.
- Use `**+= 1**` to increment the values by 1.

Useful tip:

- You can use this technique to update values for other operations, such as subtraction or multiplication.

What to remember:

- Dictionaries are mutable so that you can modify their values in place.
- This approach works for incrementing values in any dictionary.

65. Converting a list to a string

You can easily convert a list into a string in Python. This is useful when you want to present your list as a single, well-formatted string. Here's how to do it:

Program code:

```
fruits = ['apple', 'orange', 'mango', 'papaya', 'guava']
listAsString = ' '.join(fruits)
print(listAsString)
```

What to pay attention to:

- Use the `.join` function to convert the list to a string.
- The function takes the list as an argument and joins its elements with the specified separator (in this case, a space).
- The result is a single string with list elements separated by the chosen separator.

What to remember:

- The order of elements in the resulting string is the same as in the original list.
- You can use any separator you like within the `.join()` function (e.g., a comma or a hyphen).

Useful tip:

- This technique is handy when you want to create a comma-separated or space-separated string from a list, which is commonly needed in various data manipulation tasks.

66. How to convert a list to a tuple in Python?

Converting a list to a tuple is a handy operation in Python. It can be achieved using the **`tuple()`** function. However, it's important to remember that tuples are immutable, which means you can't convert them back to lists.

Program code:

```
#Let's say you have a list of fruits:
fruits = ['apple', 'orange', 'mango', 'papaya', 'guava']

# To convert this list into a tuple, you can use the `tuple()` function as shown below:
list_as_tuple = tuple(fruits)

# Now, `list_as_tuple` contains the same elements as your original list, but in tuple format. You can print it to see the result:
print(list_as_tuple)
```

Output:

```
('apple', 'orange', 'mango', 'papaya', 'guava')
```

What to remember:

- Converting a list to a tuple is a one-way operation, and the resulting tuple is immutable, meaning you can't modify its elements once it's created. This can be useful when you want to ensure that your data remains constant and can't be accidentally changed in your program.

67. How do you count the occurrences of a particular element in the list?

To count how many times a specific element appears in a Python list, you can use the `**count()**` function. It's a handy way to keep track of elements in your lists.

Here's a practical example:

Program code:

```
fruits = ['apple', 'orange', 'mango', 'papaya', 'guava']
apple_count = fruits.count('apple')
print("The count of 'apple' in the list is:", apple_count)
```

Output:

```
1
```

Useful tip:

- This is a quick and efficient way to find the frequency of elements in your lists, especially when you need to analyze data.

What to remember:

- The `**count()**` function takes one argument, which is the element you want to count. It returns the number of times that element appears in the list.

68. How do you sort a list in Python?

Sorting a list in Python is a common task, and you have a few options to choose from. Let's explore them, along with some tips for each method.

1. Using the `sort` method:

You can sort a list in-place using the `**sort**` method.

Here's how it's done:

Program code:

```
my_list = [3, 4, 1, 2]
my_list.sort()
```

Useful tip:

- This method modifies the original list and doesn't create a new one.

2. Using the `sorted` function:

If you prefer not to modify the original list, you can use the `**sorted**` function, which returns a new sorted list:

Program code:

```
my_list = [3, 4, 1, 2]
sorted_list = sorted(my_list)
```

Useful tip:

- The `**sorted**` function is a great choice when you want to keep the original list intact.

3. Using the `sort` function from the `operator` module:

For more advanced sorting needs, you can use the `**sorted**` function with a custom key function from the `**operator**` module. This allows you to sort lists of dictionaries, for instance:

Program code:
```
from operator import itemgetter

my_list = [{"a": 3}, {"a": 1}, {"a": 2}]
sorted_list = sorted(my_list, key=itemgetter("a"))
```

Useful tip:

- This is handy when you need to sort a list of complex objects based on a specific attribute or key.

What to remember:

- Choosing the right sorting method depends on your specific needs, whether you want to sort in-place, create a new sorted list, or perform custom sorting based on specific criteria.

69. How do you create a dictionary in Python?

Creating a dictionary in Python is a breeze and offers various methods to suit your preferences.

Here are three easy ways to get started:

1. Curly Braces and Colons:

The most common method is to use curly braces to define a dictionary and separate keys and values with colons.

Program code:
```
my_dict = {"key1": "value1", "key2": "value2"}
```

What to remember:

- Enclose the entire dictionary in curly braces `**{}**`.
- Separate keys and values with colons `**:**`.

2. Using the `dict` function:

You can also utilize the `**dict**` function, specifying key-value pairs as arguments.

Program code:
```
my_dict = dict(key1="value1", key2="value2")
```

Useful tips:

- Avoid using spaces in the key names.
- Use the `**dict**` function when you want to create a dictionary dynamically.

3. Using the `dict` constructor:

Alternatively, you can employ the `**dict**` constructor to build a dictionary by passing a sequence of key-value pairs using tuples within a list.

Program code:

```
my_dict = dict([("key1", "value1"), ("key2", "value2")])
```

Useful tip:

- This method is useful when you have your data organized in a list or another iterable.

What to remember:

- Creating dictionaries in Python is a fundamental skill, and you'll use them frequently in your programming journey. Choose the method that fits your needs and coding style, and start storing and retrieving data efficiently!

Functions and Classes

70. What are functions in Python?

Functions in Python are like little blocks of organized and reusable code designed to perform specific tasks or actions. They play a vital role in creating better modularity for applications by enabling the reuse of code, which enhances the overall efficiency of a program.

In Python, you'll find a variety of built-in functions readily available, such as print(), that serve specific purposes. Moreover, Python provides the flexibility to create your own functions, known as user-defined functions. This feature empowers developers to tailor functions to their specific needs and craft efficient and easy-to-maintain code.

Mastering the concept of functions is essential for any Python programmer, as it allows you to break down complex problems into smaller, manageable pieces, making your code more organized and easier to understand. When you encounter repetitive tasks in your code, functions come to the rescue, as they enable you to avoid redundant code and promote code reusability.

71. How do you define functions in Python?

In Python, defining functions is a fundamental skill that empowers you to organize and reuse your code effectively.

Syntax:

```
def function_name(parameters):
    # Function body
    # Your code here
    return result  # Optional
```

Program code:

```
def greet(name):
    return f"Hello, {name}!"

# Call the function
print(greet("Alice"))
```

What to pay attention to:
- Use a clear and descriptive name for your function.
- Parameters are values that the function takes as inputs.
- The function body contains the code to execute.
- `return` statement is optional; it specifies the value the function produces.

Useful tips:
- Aim for functions that perform a specific task.
- Reusability is key; the design functions to be versatile.

What to remember:
- Indentation is crucial; it defines the scope of the function.
- Functions are not executed until called.

72. Explain the difference between arguments and parameters

In Python, the terms "arguments" and "parameters" are often used interchangeably, but they serve distinct roles in the programming world. Let's break down their differences with practical examples to ensure a solid understanding.

Parameters

Parameters are the placeholders in a function definition. They act as variables that define the input a function expects. Think of them as labels awaiting values when the function is called. For instance:

Program code:
```
def greet(name):
    print("Hello, " + name + "!")
```

In this example, `name` is a parameter. When you call the function `greet("Alice")`, "Alice" is passed as an argument to the `name` parameter, and the function prints "Hello, Alice!".

What to remember:
- Parameters are defined in the function signature and act as placeholders.
- They specify the type and order of values a function expects.

Arguments

Conversely, arguments are the actual values passed to a function when it is called. Going back to our `greet` example:

Program code:

```
greet("Bob")
```

Here, "Bob" is the argument. It gets assigned to the `name` parameter inside the `greet` function, and the function prints "Hello, Bob!".

What to pay attention to:

- The number and order of arguments must match the parameters defined in the function.
- Arguments provide the actual data that the function processes.

Useful tips:

- Python supports various ways of passing arguments, such as positional, keyword, and default arguments.
- Pay attention to the function's documentation to understand the expected arguments.

Parameters are like signposts in a function, indicating the type and order of expected values, while arguments are the real data that fulfill those expectations when the function is called.

73. What are *args and **kwargs?

- ***args** is used when we want to pass a variable number of non-keyword arguments to a function. It collects them into a tuple.
- ****kwargs**, on the other hand, is employed for handling variable numbers of keyword arguments. It collects them into a dictionary.

Note: While ***args** and ****kwargs** are conventional names, you can use any names you find more meaningful.

****When to use *args and **kwargs:**

- ***args** is handy for functions where the number of arguments may vary. For example, if you have a function that adds any number of values together, ***args** is a great choice.
- ****kwargs** is best suited for methods with a limited scope, such as private methods (those starting with an underscore) used in specific places within a class.

***args:** use when dealing with an uncertain number of non-keyword arguments.

Program code:
```
def add_values(*args):
    return sum(args)
```

****kwargs:** ideal for managing a variable number of keyword arguments, especially in methods with a focused scope.

Program code:
```
def process_data(**kwargs):
    for key, value in kwargs.items():
        print(f"{key}: {value}")
```

Useful tips:

- Private methods: reserve ****kwargs** for private methods with limited usage within a class, such as those marked by an underscore. Avoid using it extensively across multiple classes.
- Code maintainability: while ***args** and ****kwargs** provide flexibility, be mindful of code maintainability. Excessive use can make code harder to understand.

74. How do you return multiple values from a function?

You can return multiple values from a function using a tuple in Python. This allows you to pack and unpack different data types efficiently.

Program code:
```
def get_coordinates():
    x = 10
    y = 20
    z = 30
    return x, y, z

# Call the function and unpack the returned values
result_x, result_y, result_z = get_coordinates()

# Now you can use these values as needed
print(f"X: {result_x}, Y: {result_y}, Z: {result_z}")
```

What to pay attention to:

- The multiple values are packed into a tuple using the `**return x, y, z**` syntax.
- When calling the function, you can unpack the returned values directly into variables.

Useful tips:

- You can also return other data types like lists or dictionaries.
- If the number of values is fixed, unpacking can be done in a single line for simplicity.
- Use an underscore (_) as a placeholder if you want to ignore a specific value.

For example _, result_y, _ = get_coordinates() if you only care about the second value.

- Embrace Tuple Unpacking to simplify your code and make it more expressive.

What to remember:

- Order matters when unpacking. Ensure the variables match the order of the returned values.
- Tuples are immutable, meaning their values cannot be changed after creation.

75. What is recursion?

Recursion is a fascinating concept in programming! It's all about a function calling itself, either once or multiple times, within its own body. It's like a function that plays a game of "mirror, mirror on the wall" with itself!

But here's the thing: we need to be careful when using recursion in our programs. There's one crucial condition it must fulfill - the function should have a way to stop calling itself eventually. Otherwise, we might end up stuck in an infinite loop, and that's no fun for anyone!

So, when using recursion, we need to ensure that the function's logic includes a termination condition. That way, it knows when to stop calling itself and gracefully concludes its task.

76. What is the purpose of \`len()\` in Python?

In Python, the \`**len()**\` function is like a handy measuring tape for your data. It helps you figure out how long things are, whether it's a word, a list of items, or more.

Here's a quick example to make it crystal clear:

Program code:

```
text = "helloPython"
length = len(text)
print(length)
```

Output:

```
11
```

In this case, `**len()**` told us that the word "helloPython" has 11 characters in it. Super useful when you need to work with data of varying lengths!

77. What is the `bytes()` function?

The `**bytes()**` function in Python is pretty nifty! It helps us convert objects into bytes objects or create empty bytes objects of a specific size.

Let's break it down a bit: When you use the `**bytes()**` function, it takes an object (like a string or a list) and converts it into a bytes object. This can be super useful when you're working with binary data or dealing with data that needs to be stored efficiently.

And guess what? The `**bytes()**` function can do more! If you want to create an empty bytes object with a specific size, you can pass in the desired size as an argument, and it will create the empty bytes object for you. This is great for allocating memory or working with binary data structures.

Here's an example demonstrating the usage of the `**bytes()**` function in Python:

Program code:

```
# Example 1: Converting objects into bytes objects
string_data = "Hello, Python!"
bytes_data = bytes(string_data, 'utf-8')

print(f"Original string: {string_data}")
print(f"Converted bytes: {bytes_data}")

# Example 2: Creating empty bytes objects of a specified size
empty_bytes = bytes(5)
print(f"Empty bytes of size 5: {empty_bytes}")
```

Output:

```
Original string: Hello, Python!
Converted bytes: b'Hello, Python!'
Empty bytes of size 5: b'\x00\x00\x00\x00\x00'
```

In the first example, we convert the string "Hello, Python!" into a bytes object using the `**bytes()**` function with the `**'utf-8'**` encoding. The `**b'Hello, Python!'**` represents the bytes object.

In the second example, we create an empty bytes object of size 5 by passing the size (5 in this case) as an argument to the `**bytes()**` function. The resulting bytes object `**b'\x00\x00\x00\x00\x00'**` consists of five null bytes since we didn't provide any initial data.

These are just a few use cases of the `**bytes()**` function, and it can be particularly handy when dealing with binary data, network communications, and more.

78. What is a `map()` function in Python?

The `**map()**` function in Python is a handy tool that allows you to apply a specific function to each element in a given collection (like a list, tuple, or any other iterable). It's a powerful way to perform the same operation on multiple items without writing repetitive code.

How does the `map()` function work?
The `**map()**` function takes two parameters:
- A function: This is the operation you want to perform on each element of the iterable.
- An iterable: This is the collection of items on which the function will be applied.

The function you provide is then executed on each element of the iterable, and the result is collected into a new iterator, which you can convert into a list or use in other ways.
Example: Let's say we want to double each number in a tuple. We'll define a simple function called `**double_num()**` that takes a number as input and returns its double:

Program code:
```
def double_num(n):
    return n + n

numbers = (15, 25, 35, 45)
result = map(double_num, numbers)

# To see the output, we can convert the result into a list
output_list = list(result)
print(output_list)
```

Output:
```
[30, 50, 70, 90]
```

In this example, the `**map()**` function applies the `**double_num()**` function to each element of the `**numbers**` tuple. As a result, it returns a new iterator containing the doubled values, which we then convert into a list and print the output.

79. What is the `type()` in Python?

In Python, the `**type()**` function is a handy tool that helps us figure out the data type of an object or even create a new object with a specified type. It's a useful tool for beginners and experienced developers alike.

Program code:

```
# Let's define a variable 'a' and assign it the value 100
a = 100

# Now, let's use the type() function to check its data type
result = type(a)

# Print the result
print(result)
```

Output:

```
<class 'int'>
```

In this example, we've created a variable `**a**` and set it to 100. Then, we used the `**type()**` function to check its data type. In the output, we see that it returns `**<class 'int'>**`, which means the data type of `**a**` is an integer.

So, whether you're examining the data type of an existing variable or creating a new one, the `**type()**` function is your friend in Python. It's a simple yet powerful tool that helps you understand and work with different data types effectively.

80. What is the `split()` function in Python?

The `**split()**` function in Python is a handy tool that lets you divide a string into smaller pieces, or substrings, based on specific separators. This can be incredibly useful when you have a long string and want to extract individual elements or words from it.

Program code:

```
text = "A, B, C"
letters = text.split(", ")
print(letters)
```

Output:

```
['A', 'B', 'C']
```

In this example, we've taken a string containing letters separated by commas and used the `**split()**` function to create a list of individual letters. The `**", "**` argument passed to `**split()**` specifies that the separator is a comma followed by a space. The result is a list (`**letters**`) that contains `**['A', 'B', 'C']**`. This can be extremely useful for parsing data, processing user input, or breaking down text into manageable parts.

81. What is `slice()` in Python?

Slicing in Python is a fundamental concept that allows you to extract specific portions of a sequence, which can be any iterable object like strings, lists, or tuples. It's a handy tool to access the elements you need. Python provides the `**slice()**` function to perform slicing, and there are two ways to use it:

1. Slice(start, stop)

This form of slicing extracts elements from the `**start**` index up to, but not including, the `**stop**` index. For example:

Program code:

```
my_list = [1, 2, 3, 4, 5]
my_slice = slice(1, 4)
result = my_list[my_slice]  # Extracts elements at indices 1, 2, and 3
print(result)  # Output: [2, 3, 4]
```

2. Slice(start, stop, step)

In this variation, you can also specify a `**step**` parameter, which determines the stride between elements to be included. It allows you to skip elements as you slice. For example:

Program code:

```
my_string = "PythonIsFun"
my_slice = slice(0, 12, 2)
result = my_string[my_slice] # Extracts characters at even indices
print(result) # Output: "PtoIFn"
```

Program code:

```
my_list = [1, 2, 3, 4, 5]
result = my_list[1:4] # Equivalent to using a slice object
print(result)
```

Output:

```
[2, 3, 4]
```

Useful tip:

- You can also use a concise slice notation directly within square brackets, like this:

What to remember:

- The `**start**` index is inclusive, while the `**stop**` index is exclusive.
- Slicing is versatile and works with various data types.
- Be mindful of index boundaries to avoid IndexError.

Slicing is a powerful technique that simplifies data manipulation in Python, and once you get the hang of it, you'll find it incredibly useful in many situations.

82. Lambda functions in Python

What is a Lambda Function?

A lambda function is a small, anonymous function in Python. It can have any number of arguments but can only have one expression. The expression is evaluated and returned when the function is called. Lambda functions are typically used for short operations that are simple enough to be described in a single line of code.

Let's say you want to find the sum of all elements in the list `**[5, 8, 10, 20, 50, 100]**`.

Using a lambda function, this can be achieved as follows:

Program code:

```
numbers = [5, 8, 10, 20, 50, 100]
sum_of_elements = lambda x: sum(x)
print(sum_of_elements(numbers))
```

When you run this code, it will print `**193**`, which is the sum of all the elements in the list.

Useful tip:

- While lambda functions are powerful and concise, remember not to overuse them. If the operation becomes too complex, it's often clearer to define a regular function instead.

What to remember:

- Lambda functions are also known as anonymous functions.
- They can take multiple arguments.
- Only a single expression can be used inside them.
- They are typically used for short, simple operations.

83. Generating random numbers in Python

To create random numbers in Python, we rely on the versatile `**random**` module. It's a handy tool for all sorts of randomness. Let's dive into a couple of practical examples to get you started.

Generating a random floating-point number (between 0 and 1)
If you need a random decimal between 0 and 1.

Program code:

```
import random
n = random.random()
print(n)
```

Generating a random integer within a specified range
Sometimes, you may want a random integer within a specific range, like between `**a**` and `**b**`.

Program code:

```
import random
n = random.randint(a, b)
print(n)
```

Useful tips:

- Remember to import the `**random**` module at the beginning of your script.

- Use `**random.random()**` for floating-point numbers and `**random.randint(a, b)**` for integers.
- Be sure to specify the range when using `**random.randint(a, b)**`.

Random numbers can add an element of unpredictability to your Python programs, making them more dynamic and versatile.

Modules, Packages and Libraries

84. What is PIP, and how do you use it?

PIP, short for Preferred Installer Program, is a handy tool that simplifies the process of installing and managing third-party libraries in Python. Let's explore some essential tasks you can perform with PIP, along with practical examples:

Installing Packages:

- Command: `**pip install package_name**`
- Example: `**pip install requests**`
- Tip: Always ensure you have the correct package name, and consider using a virtual environment to keep dependencies isolated.

Specifying Versions:

- Command: `**pip install package_name==version**`
- Example: `**pip install requests==2.25.0**`
- Remember: Specifying versions ensures compatibility, especially when working on projects with specific library versions.

Upgrading Packages:

- Command: `**pip install --upgrade package_name**`
- Example: `**pip install --upgrade requests**`
- Tip: Regularly update packages to benefit from bug fixes, new features, and security patches.

Uninstalling Packages:

- Command: `**pip uninstall package_name**`
- Example: `**pip uninstall requests**`
- Pay attention: Uninstalling a package removes it from your environment, so use it cautiously.

Listing Installed Packages:

- Command: `**pip list**`
- Example: `**pip list**`
- Useful tip: Periodically check your installed packages to stay informed about versions and dependencies.

Installing from requirements.txt:
- Command: `pip install -r requirements.txt`
- Example: `pip install -r requirements.txt`
- Handy tip: Maintain a clear and organized requirements.txt file to streamline collaboration and deployment.

Note for Older Python Versions:
If you're using a Python version older than 3.3, you might need to install PIP separately. Most modern systems come with PIP pre-installed, but it's good to double-check.

85. What are Python modules?

Python modules are like toolboxes that help organize and group related Python commands, functions, classes, and variables into a single file. It's like having a neatly labeled container for all the code you need! This approach makes your code easier to understand and maintain.

Think of modules as little packages of functionality that you can import into your Python programs whenever you need them. By breaking down your code into modules, you keep things logically organized, making it simpler to navigate and use.

For instance, let's say you have a bunch of functions and classes related to handling user authentication. By placing them in a module called "user_auth", you can easily import and reuse them across different projects without copying and pasting code all over the place.

Using modules also promotes code reusability, making your programming journey more efficient and enjoyable. So, embrace the power of Python modules, and you'll be on your way to writing cleaner, well-organized, and more maintainable code!

86. What are packages in Python?

Packages in Python are a way to organize related modules into a single directory hierarchy. Think of them as folders containing multiple Python files, making managing and structuring your code easier.

Imagine you're building a web application and need functionality for handling user authentication, database operations, and sending emails. Instead of cramming all the code into one file, you can create separate packages for authentication, database, and email modules.

What to pay attention to:

- Import statements: When using packages, you'll often need to use import statements to access modules within them. Remember the correct syntax, such as `**import package.module**`.
- Folder Structure: Maintain a logical hierarchy within your package. It helps to keep related modules together, enhancing code readability.

Useful tips:

- Choose meaningful names for your packages, reflecting their purpose.
- Keep your packages small and focused on specific functionalities to promote code maintainability.

What to remember:

- Packages are a way to organize code and make it modular.
- They prevent naming conflicts by encapsulating module names within their namespace.

If you write a large Python program, using packages can significantly simplify your code structure.

87. What are libraries in Python?

In Python, libraries are powerful tools that simplify coding tasks by providing pre-written functions and modules. Think of them as ready-made toolboxes stocked with useful functions and features. Let's delve into why libraries are crucial, offering practical insights for beginners.

Why Are Libraries Important?

Libraries save time and effort by offering pre-built functions, sparing you from reinventing the wheel. They cover various functionalities, from handling data to implementing complex algorithms. For instance, the 'math' library simplifies mathematical operations, while 'requests' facilitates web interactions.

Consider the '**random**' library. Instead of creating your own logic for generating random numbers, you can import the 'random' library and use its functions.

Program code:

```
import random

random_number = random.randint(1, 100)
print(random_number)
```

What to pay attention to:

- When using libraries, be mindful of compatibility. Ensure that your library version is compatible with your Python version. This is especially important as libraries are continuously updated.

Useful tip:

- Explore community-supported libraries like NumPy for scientific computing or requests for handling HTTP requests. These libraries often come with vibrant communities, making problem-solving more accessible.

What to remember:

- Python's extensive standard library is a goldmine for beginners. Familiarize yourself with it, as it provides a broad spectrum of functionalities, from file handling ('os' library) to regular expressions ('re' library).

Libraries in Python are your coding companions, streamlining tasks and expanding your capabilities. Embrace them to enhance your coding efficiency, but always stay vigilant about compatibility and explore the vast standard library for built-in functionalities.

88. What are the popular packages and libraries for data manipulation in Python?

In the vast world of Python, several libraries stand out for their prowess in data manipulation. These tools are crucial for anyone diving into data science or analysis. Let's explore popular libraries that can supercharge your data manipulation skills.

Pandas: The powerhouse of data manipulation, Pandas excels in handling and analyzing structured data.

NumPy: This library is a cornerstone for numerical operations, supporting large, multi-dimensional arrays and matrices.

SciPy: This is a powerful Python library for scientific computing that builds on NumPy, providing additional functionality for optimization, integration, interpolation, eigenvalue problems, and more.

Matplotlib: Visualize your data with Matplotlib's extensive plotting capabilities, perfect for creating insightful charts and graphs.

Seaborn: Built on top of Matplotlib, Seaborn adds a layer of style and simplicity to enhance your visualizations.

Scikit-learn: Dive into machine learning effortlessly with Scikit-learn, offering classification, regression, clustering, and more tools.

Statsmodels: If statistical models are your focus, Statsmodels is your go-to library for estimating and testing hypotheses.

Beautiful Soup: Web scraping made easy – Beautiful Soup helps parse HTML and XML documents effortlessly.

Requests: Simplifying HTTP requests, Requests is a versatile library for interacting with APIs and fetching data from the web.

SQLAlchemy: SQLAlchemy provides a powerful and flexible SQL toolkit for database interaction.

TensorFlow: Delve into deep learning with TensorFlow, an open-source machine learning framework.

Keras: A high-level neural networks API, Keras simplifies building and experimenting with neural networks.

NLTK (Natural Language Toolkit): Process and analyze human language data with NLTK's comprehensive set of libraries and programs.

Scrapy: Take web scraping to the next level with Scrapy, a fast and efficient framework for extracting data from websites.

Plotly: Elevate your interactive visualizations with Plotly, offering dynamic and responsive charts.

Bokeh: Another powerful visualization library, Bokeh specializes in creating interactive plots for the web.

GeoPandas: If geographical data is your focus, GeoPandas extends Pandas to handle spatial data seamlessly.

Folium: Visualize geospatial data on interactive leaflet maps using Folium – perfect for exploration and analysis.

PyTorch: A dynamic neural network library, PyTorch is widely used for deep learning and research.

OpenCV: Dive into computer vision with OpenCV, an open-source library that supports real-time image processing.

NetworkX: Explore the world of complex networks and graphs with NetworkX, a versatile library for studying structure and dynamics.

89. Describe Python's module system and how to create and use modules

In Python, modules are like toolkits that help you organize and structure your code. They allow you to break down your program into smaller, manageable pieces, making your code more modular and easier to maintain. Here's a beginner-friendly guide to Python's module system, along with practical examples and essential tips to keep in mind.

What are modules?
Think of modules as containers for Python code. They consist of functions, variables, and classes bundled together to perform a specific task.

Creating your module:
1. Begin by writing your code in a separate Python file, for example, `**my_module.py**`.
2. Define functions, variables, or classes within the file.
3. Save the file in the same directory as your main program.

Using modules in your code:
1. To use a module, import it using the `**import**` keyword.

Program code:
```
import my_module
```

2. Access functions or variables from the module using dot notation.

Program code:
```
my_module.my_function()
```

Example 1: Creating a module

Program code:

```
# my_module.py
def greet(name):
    return f"Hello, {name}!"

# main_program.py
import my_module

print(my_module.greet("John"))
```

Example 2: Using module variables

Program code:

```
# my_module.py
pi = 3.1416

# main_program.py
import my_module

radius = 5
area = my_module.pi * (radius ** 2)
print(f"Area of the circle: {area}")
```

Tips and reminders:

- **Keep it clean:** Break down your code into logical modules, each serving a specific purpose. This enhances readability and maintainability.
- **Mind your names:** Choose a clear and concise alias when importing a module throughout your code. For instance:

Program code:

```
import my_module as mm
```

- **Avoid circular imports:** Be cautious of circular dependencies, where modules depend on each other. This can lead to unexpected behavior.
- **Check standard library:** Python comes with a rich standard library. Before reinventing the wheel, explore available modules to save time and effort.

90. What's the difference between packages and modules?

In Python, packages and modules play distinct roles in organizing and structuring code. Let's break down the differences.

Python module:

Think of a module as a standalone file that houses Python code. It encapsulates functions, variables, and other elements vital to your program. Modules group related code into separate files, promoting code organization and enhancing reusability.

Program code:

```
# Example module: math_operations.py

def add(a, b):
    return a + b

def subtract(a, b):
    return a - b
```

Python package:

On the other hand, packages are like bundles of code, housing multiple modules and possibly sub-packages. This structure aids in organizing related modules within a single directory.

```
project_directory/
|-- package_name/
|   |-- module1.py
|   |-- module2.py
|   |-- subpackage/
|       |-- module3.py
```

What to pay attention to:

- Modules are individual files, while packages are directories containing multiple modules.
- Modules help in code organization and reusability.
- Packages are crucial for managing larger projects with diverse functionalities.

Useful tips:

- Use modules to keep related functions and variables together.
- Employ packages for better organization, especially in extensive projects.
- Remember that a package can have both modules and sub-packages.

91. What's the difference between modules, packages, libraries, and frameworks?

Python modules

To keep your code organized, start by creating modules. A module is a collection of related code stored in a file with a .py extension. You can define functions, classes, or variables in a module.

Remember, you can import specific functions from a module, enhancing code readability.

Python packages

As your application grows, managing numerous modules becomes challenging. Enter packages, which are directories containing related modules. To be recognized as a package, a directory must include an __init__.py file. Organize your modules into packages and subpackages for a hierarchical structure.

Packages provide a crucial organizational structure as your Python project expands.

Python libraries

Libraries encompass reusable code chunks, often used interchangeably with packages. They consist of related modules and packages. Developers create libraries to share code with the community, eliminating the need to start from scratch. Examples include NumPy, Pandas, Matplotlib, and PyTorch.

Python frameworks

Frameworks, more complex than libraries, provide a foundation and architecture for applications. Django, Flask, and Bottle are popular Python frameworks, offering essential building blocks for developers. Think of frameworks as the blueprint for your application, streamlining development and ensuring a consistent structure.

Exception Handling and Debugging

92. How do you debug a Python program?

Debugging a Python program is a crucial skill to master. Here are some beginner-friendly ways to debug your Python code:

1. The trusty print statement:

- One of the simplest methods is using the `**print**` statement. You can insert `**print**` statements in your code to display variable values and intermediate results in the console. For example:

Program code:

```
x = 5
print("The value of x is:", x)
```

- Keep an eye on the console for these printouts. They can help you understand what's happening in your program step by step.

2. Using debuggers:

- Python has powerful built-in debuggers like `**pdb**` or the more user-friendly `**ipdb**`. You can insert breakpoints in your code and examine variables interactively.

- To use `**ipdb**`, make sure to install it first (`**pip install ipdb**`). Then, you can add this line where you want to break:

Program code:

```
import ipdb; ipdb.set_trace()
```

- Run your program, and it will stop at the breakpoint, allowing you to inspect variables and step through your code.

3. Assert statements:

- Another useful technique is adding `**assert**` statements in your code. These checks can ensure certain conditions hold true during program execution. If the condition is false, it raises an `**AssertionError**`, helping you catch issues early.

Program code:

```
x = 10
assert x > 0, "x must be greater than 0"
```

- If `x` is not greater than 0, you'll get an error message guiding you to the problematic part of your code.

What to remember:

- Debugging is your ally when things don't go as planned. Start with `print` statements, explore debuggers like `ipdb`, and use `assert` statements to catch issues. Keep a watchful eye on your code, and you'll become a debugging pro quickly!

93. How do you handle exceptions in Python?

When writing Python code, it's important to anticipate and handle exceptions gracefully. Here's a simple and effective way to do it using a try-except block.

Program code:

```
try:
    # code that may raise an exception
except SomeExceptionType:
    # code to handle the exception
```

What to pay attention to:

- Try Block: This is where you place the code that might raise an exception. It's where the action happens.
- Except Block: Here, you specify what should be done if an exception occurs. You can provide specific handling for different exception types.

Useful tips:

- Be as specific as possible when catching exceptions. This allows you to handle different exceptions differently, making your code more robust.
- Always include helpful error messages in your exception handling code. This aids debugging and makes it easier to identify issues.
- Avoid using a broad `except` clause that catches all exceptions. It can make debugging harder.

What to remember:

- You can handle various types of exceptions by specifying different `SomeExceptionType` in the `except` block.

- Exception handling prevents your program from crashing when unexpected issues occur.

Handling exceptions is a fundamental skill in Python programming. It ensures your code runs smoothly even when it encounters unexpected situations.

94. What is the purpose of `raise` in exception handling?

Exception handling is a crucial aspect of writing robust Python code, and the "raise" keyword plays a key role in this process. So, what's the purpose of "raise," and how can it elevate your coding skills?

Understanding the basics:
In Python, exceptions are events that disrupt the normal flow of your program. When an issue occurs, an exception is raised. The "raise" keyword allows you to raise exceptions in your code deliberately.

Practical example:
Consider this scenario – you're developing a function that calculates the square root of a number. To ensure that the input is a positive number, you can use "raise" to trigger a specific exception if the condition is not met.

Program code:
```
def calculate_square_root(number):
    if number < 0:
        raise ValueError("Input must be a non-negative number")
    # Rest of the code for square root calculation
```

What to pay attention to:
- Use "raise" to indicate that something unexpected or undesirable has occurred.
- Specify the type of exception you're raising, like ValueError in the example above.
- Provide a clear and informative error message to aid debugging.

Useful tips:
- Don't overuse "raise"; reserve it for exceptional cases.
- Be specific with exception types to enhance clarity in your code.

What to remember:

- "raise" helps you control the flow of your program by signaling exceptions.
- It's a powerful tool for making your code more robust and user-friendly.

The "raise" keyword empowers you to handle exceptions gracefully, guiding your program through unexpected situations. By incorporating it wisely, you enhance the reliability and readability of your Python code.

95. Explain the importance of debugging in Python

Debugging is a crucial skill for any Python developer, helping you identify and fix errors in your code. It's like being a detective, solving mysteries in your program. Let's dive into why debugging is important and how to master this skill.

Why debugging matters

- **Spotting mistakes:** Debugging allows you to catch and correct mistakes in your code. Even the most experienced developers rely on debugging tools to find elusive errors.

- **Saving time:** Identifying and fixing bugs early in the development process saves you time in the long run. It prevents issues from snowballing into bigger problems later.

Practical tips for effective debugging

1. Use print() statements: A simple yet powerful way to trace your code is by strategically placing print statements. This helps you see the values of variables at different points in your program.

Program code:
```
def example_function(x, y):
    print(f"x: {x}, y: {y}")
    result = x + y
    print(f"Result: {result}")
    return result
```

2. Leverage integrated development environments (IDEs): IDEs like PyCharm and VSCode have built-in debugging tools. Set breakpoints, step through code, and inspect variables to understand what's happening under the hood.

3. Use assertions: Incorporate assertions to check if certain conditions hold true at specific points in your code. This helps catch issues early in development.

Program code:

```
def calculate_area(radius):
    assert radius > 0, "Radius must be positive"
    return 3.14 * radius * radius
```

Key takeaways:

- **Patience is key:** Debugging can be challenging, but stay patient. It's a skill that improves with practice.
- **Learn your tools:** Familiarize yourself with the debugging features in your chosen IDE. Knowing how to use breakpoints, watch variables, and step through code will make your debugging sessions more effective.
- **Document your process:** Document your debugging process if you're working on a complex issue. This helps you keep track and serves as a reference for future problem-solving.

Remember, every developer encounters bugs. It's not about avoiding them entirely but about becoming skilled at finding and fixing them efficiently.

96. What tools are available for debugging Python code?

Debugging is a crucial skill for any Python developer. Here, we'll explore some essential tools to help you identify and fix issues in your code.

1. print() statements:

The simplest way to debug is using `**print()**` statements. Insert them strategically in your code to display variable values and trace the flow.

Program code:

```
def multiply(a, b):
    result = a * b
    print(f"{a} * {b} = {result}")
    return result
```

2. pdb (Python debugger):

Python comes with a built-in debugger, `**pdb**`. Insert `**import pdb; pdb.set_trace()**` where you suspect issues for an interactive debugging session.

Navigate through code execution step by step with commands like `n` (next) and `c` (continue).

3. Logging:

The `logging` module helps you log messages with different severity levels. Use it to record the program's behavior.

Adjust logging levels (`DEBUG`, `INFO`, `WARNING`, `ERROR`, `CRITICAL`) to focus on specific aspects of your code.

4. IDE Features:

Most Integrated Development Environments (IDEs) have powerful debugging features. Set breakpoints, inspect variables, and step through your code.

In **VS Code** or **PyCharm**, use the debugger by setting breakpoints and utilizing the debugging toolbar.

5. Assertions:

Integrate `assert` statements to enforce assumptions about your code. If an assertion fails, it indicates an issue.

Use assertions for both testing and debugging purposes.

6. Third-Party Tools:

Tools like `pdb++`, and `ipdb` offer additional features and a more user.

97. How do you handle common debugging scenarios?

Navigating through common debugging scenarios in Python is crucial for a smooth coding experience. Let's dive into practical tips and examples that can guide beginners through these challenges:

1. Understanding tracebacks:

When encountering an error, the traceback provides valuable information. Pay attention to the last line, which points to the specific file and line where the error occurred.

For example:

```
File "script.py", line 5, in <module>
  result = divide(10, 0)
ZeroDivisionError: division by zero
```

Focus on the error type (e.g., `**ZeroDivisionError**`) and the location (e.g., `**line 5**`).

2. Print statements for quick insight:

Introduce print statements strategically to narrow down where the issue arises.

Program code:

```
def divide(x, y):
    print(f'Dividing {x} by {y}')
    result = x / y
    return result
```

3. Using debugger tools:

Leverage Python's built-in debugger, `**pdb**`, for a more systematic approach. Insert the following line where you suspect the problem:

Program code:

```
import pdb; pdb.set_trace()
```

Run your script, and it will pause execution at that point, allowing you to inspect variables and step through the code.

4. Check variable values:

Sometimes, unexpected values can be the root cause. Ensure your variables contain what you expect by printing or using the debugger.

5. Handling exceptions:

Anticipate potential errors by using try-except blocks. This prevents your program from crashing and allows for graceful error handling:

Program code:

```
try:
    result = divide(10, 0)
except ZeroDivisionError as e:
    print(f"Error: {e}")
```

6. Remember to undo recent changes:

If the error seems to be related to recent modifications, consider undoing those changes to identify the root cause.

7. Consult documentation and online resources:

Don't hesitate to consult Python's official documentation or online communities like Stack Overflow. Others might have encountered similar issues and can offer insights.

8. Keep calm and stay persistent:

Debugging is a natural part of coding, even for experienced developers. Stay patient, break down the problem, and tackle it step by step.

Python Patterns

98. Print the following pattern #1

This is a standard Python interview question that tests your understanding of nested loops.

Pattern:

```
1
2 2
3 3 3
4 4 4 4
5 5 5 5 5
```

You can achieve this pattern using nested loops. Pay attention to the logic, and remember to include a new line after each row to display the pattern correctly. Here's a step-by-step solution:

Program code:

```
# Define the total number of rows
total_rows = 5

# Outer loop to iterate through rows
for num in range(1, total_rows + 1):
    # Inner loop to print the respective numbers
    for i in range(1, num + 1):
        print(num, end=" ") # Print the number with a space
```

Code explanation:

- We use two nested loops: an outer loop to iterate through rows (from 1 to 5) and an inner loop to print the respective numbers for each row.
- The outer loop variable `**num**` represents the current row number.
- The inner loop variable `**i**` iterates from 1 to the current row number `**num**`.
- We print the value of `**num**` in the inner loop and use `**end=" "**` to separate the numbers with a space instead of a newline.

99. Print the following pattern #2

This is a standard Python interview question that tests your understanding of nested loops.

Pattern:

```
#
# #
# # #
# # # #
# # # # #
```

You can achieve this pattern using nested loops. Pay attention to the logic, and remember to include a new line after each row to display the pattern correctly. Here's a step-by-step solution:

Program code:

```
# Define the total number of rows
total_rows = 5

# Outer loop to iterate through rows
for num in range(1, total_rows + 1):
    # Inner loop to print the respective numbers
    for i in range(1, num + 1):
        print("#", end=" ")  # Print the number with a space
```

Code explanation:

- We use two nested loops: an outer loop to iterate through rows (from 1 to 5) and an inner loop to print the respective numbers for each row.
- The outer loop variable `**num**` represents the current row number.
- The inner loop variable `**i**` iterates from 1 to the current row number `**num**`.
- We print the value of `**num**` in the inner loop and use `**end=" "**` to separate the numbers with a space instead of a newline.

100. Print the following pattern #3

Pattern:

```
      #
     # #
    # # #
   # # # #
  # # # # #
 # # # # # #
# # # # # # #
```

To create this pattern, we'll use a Python function. Here's the code, and we'll break it down step by step:

Program code:

```
def print_pattern(num):
    # Define the number of spaces
    spaces = num - 1

    # Loop for each row
    for i in range(num):
        # Print spaces before the hashes
        print(" " * spaces, end="")

        # Print the hashes
        print("# " * (i + 1))

        # Decrease the number of spaces for the next row
        spaces -= 1

# Get the number of rows from the user
num = int(input("Enter the number of rows in the pattern: "))
print_pattern(num)
```

Code explanation:

- We define a function called `**print_pattern**` that takes the number of rows (`**num**`) as input.
- We initialize the `**spaces**` variable to `**num - 1**`, as we need spaces before the first hash.
- We use a loop to iterate through each row (from 0 to `**num-1**`).
- Inside the loop, we print spaces using `**" " * spaces**` to create the leading spaces.
- We then print the hashes using `**"# " * (i + 1)**` to generate the increasing number of hash

symbols in each row.

- After printing each row, we decrease the `**spaces**` variable to prepare for the next row.
- Finally, we get the number of rows from the user and call the `**print_pattern**` function to display the desired pattern.

101. Print the following pattern #4

Pattern:

```
0
0 1
0 1 2
0 1 2 3
0 1 2 3 4
```

To print this pattern, we'll use Python.

Here's the code to create the pattern:

Program code:

```
def print_pattern(rows):
    for i in range(rows):
        num = 0
        for j in range(i + 1):
            print(num, end=" ")
            num += 1
        print()

# Input the number of rows from the user
rows = int(input("Enter the number of rows in the pattern: "))
print_pattern(rows)
```

What to pay attention to:

- The `**num**` variable is initialized to 0 inside the outer loop for each row to ensure that the column starts from 0.
- The outer loop controls the number of rows, and the inner loop handles the number of columns in each row.
- We increment the `**num**` column-wise within the inner loop.

Useful tips:

- Understanding loops is essential for creating patterns like this.

- The `end=" "` parameter in the `print` function ensures that the numbers are printed on the same line with a space in between.
- Use `print()` to move to the next line after each row.

What to remember:

- You can change the pattern by modifying the starting value (`num`) and the number of rows you want to print.
- Experiment with different patterns to improve your understanding of loops in Python.

This pattern is a great exercise for beginners to practice using loops and get comfortable with Python's syntax.

102. Print the following pattern #5

Pattern:

```
1
1 2
1 2 3
1 2 3 4
1 2 3 4 5
```

Create a pattern where each row contains consecutive numbers starting from 1. The number of elements in each row increases by one.

Program code:

```
def print_pattern(rows):
    number = 1  # Initialize the starting number
    for i in range(rows):  # Loop through each row
        number = 1  # Reset the number to 1 for each row
        for j in range(i + 1):  # Loop through each column in the row
            print(number, end=" ")  # Print the number followed by a space
            number += 1  # Increment the number for the next column
        print()  # Move to the next row

# Input the number of rows for the pattern
rows = int(input("Enter the number of rows in the pattern: "))
print_pattern(rows)
```

Code explanation:

- We initialize a variable called `**number**` to 1. This variable will keep track of the numbers we print in each row.
- We use two nested loops. The outer loop iterates through each row, and the inner loop iterates through each column.
- Inside the inner loop, we print the `**number**` followed by a space. Then, we increment the `**number**` for the next column.
- After printing all the numbers in a row, we move to the next row using `**print()**` to add a new line.

Useful tips:

- Pay attention to how the `**number**` variable is used and reinitialized for each row.
- Remember to use `**end=" "` in the `print**` function to separate numbers with a space.
- You can adjust the number of rows by changing the value of `**rows**` to create different patterns.

103. Print the following pattern #6

Pattern:

```
A
B B
C C C
D D D D
```

Program code:

```
def print_character_pattern(rows):
    # Initialize the character value as 'A'
    char_value = 65

    # Outer loop handles the number of rows
    for i in range(0, rows):

        # Inner loop handles the number of columns
        for j in range(0, i + 1):

            # Convert the ASCII value to a character
            character = chr(char_value)
```

```
            # Print the character value with a space
            print(character, end=" ")

        # Increment the character value
        char_value += 1

        # Move to the next line after each row
        print("\r")

# Input: Number of rows
rows = int(input("Enter the number of rows in the pattern: "))
print_character_pattern(rows)
```

Useful tips:

- The pattern consists of rows where each row has characters from `A` to the respective row number.
- We use ASCII values to convert numbers to characters and print them.
- Pay attention to the use of nested loops for rows and columns.
- Remember to increment the character value to move from `A` to `B`, `C`, and so on.
- Use `\r` to move to the next line after each row.

This code allows you to print various character patterns by specifying the number of rows.

104. Print the following pattern #7

Pattern:

```
A
B C
D E F
G H I J
K L M N O
P Q R S T U
```

To print this pattern in Python, you can use nested loops. Here's the code to achieve it:

Program code:

```
def print_pattern(num_rows):
    char_value = 65  # ASCII value for 'A'

    for i in range(1, num_rows + 1):
        for j in range(i):
            char = chr(char_value)  # Convert ASCII value to character
            print(char, end=" ")
            char_value += 1  # Move to the next character in the alphabet
        print()  # Move to the next line for the next row

num_rows = int(input("Enter the number of rows in the pattern: "))
print_pattern(num_rows)
```

Code explanation:

- We start with the ASCII value of `**A**`, which is 65.
- We use two nested loops. The outer loop controls the number of rows, and the inner loop handles the columns.
- For each position in the pattern, we convert the current ASCII value to a character and print it.
- After each row is printed, we move to the next line using `**print()**`.

Useful tips:

- You can customize the pattern by changing the initial character or the number of rows.
- This code can be a fun way to print patterns and learn about loops and ASCII characters in Python.

Python OOP Concepts

105. What is object-oriented programming (OOP) in Python?

Object-Oriented Programming (OOP) is a powerful paradigm in Python that allows you to organize code in a more structured and modular way. Let's break it down in a beginner-friendly manner.

What is OOP?

OOP revolves around the concept of "objects" - self-contained units that bundle data and functionality. In Python, everything is an object: numbers, strings, or custom-defined classes.

Creating classes and objects:

To dive into OOP, you create classes serving as blueprints for objects. Consider a simple example:

Program code:

```
class Dog:
    def __init__(self, name, age):
        self.name = name
        self.age = age

    def bark(self):
        print(f"{self.name} says Woof!")
```

Here, we've defined a class `**Dog**` with attributes like `**name**` and `**age**`, and a method `**bark**`.

Instantiating objects:

Now, let's create instances or objects of the class:

Program code:

```
my_dog = Dog("Buddy", 3)
your_dog = Dog("Milo", 2)
```

Here, `**my_dog**` and `**your_dog**` are instances of the `**Dog**` class, each with its own set of attributes.

Accessing attributes and methods:
You can access object attributes and call methods using dot notation:

Program code:
```
print(my_dog.name) # Output: Buddy
my_dog.bark()      # Output: Buddy says Woof!
```

Inheritance:
OOP introduces inheritance, allowing a class to inherit attributes and methods from another. This promotes code reuse and simplifies maintenance:

Program code:
```
class Dachshund(Dog):
    def dig(self):
        print(f"{self.name} is digging!")

my_dachshund = Dachshund("Slinky", 1)
my_dachshund.bark()
my_dachshund.dig()
```

Output:
```
Slinky says Woof!
Slinky is digging!
```

Useful tips:
- Practice creating simple classes and objects.
- Experiment with attribute access and method invocation.
- Gradually explore more advanced OOP concepts like encapsulation and polymorphism.

What to remember:
- Objects: Fundamental building blocks, encapsulating data and functionality.
- Classes: Blueprints for creating objects.
- Attributes and Methods: Characteristics and behaviors defined within classes.
- Inheritance: Mechanism for sharing attributes and methods between classes.

106. Explain the concepts of classes and objects

In Python, classes and objects are fundamental concepts that empower you to organize and structure your code effectively. Let's break down these concepts in a way that's easy to grasp, with practical examples to guide you.

Classes: the blueprint

A class serves as a blueprint for creating objects. Think of it as a template that defines the properties and behaviors of objects. To create a class, use the `**class**` keyword, followed by a name that adheres to Python's naming conventions.

Program code:

```
class Dog:
    def __init__(self, name, age):
        self.name = name
        self.age = age

    def bark(self):
        print("Woof!")

# Creating an instance of the Dog class
my_dog = Dog("Buddy", 3)
```

Objects: instances of classes

Objects are instances of classes, created from the blueprint defined by the class. They encapsulate data and behavior. In our example, `**my_dog**` is an object of the `**Dog**` class.

Program code:

```
# Accessing object attributes
print(my_dog.name)

# Calling object methods
my_dog.bark()
```

Output:

```
Buddy
Woof!
```

Useful tips:

- **Start simple:** Begin with basic classes and gradually incorporate more complex features as you become comfortable.
- **Naming matters:** Follow Python's naming conventions for classes (CamelCase) to enhance code readability.
- **Experiment:** Create your own classes and objects to practice. The more you experiment, the better you'll understand these concepts.

What to remember:

- **Initialization Method (`__init__`):** This special method initializes object attributes. It's called automatically when you create a new object.
- **Self parameter:** The `self` parameter refers to the instance of the object itself. It's a convention in Python to use `self` as the first parameter in instance methods.
- **Encapsulation:** Encapsulating data within objects helps in organizing and structuring code, promoting modularity and reusability.

107. How do you create and initialize a class in Python?

In Python, classes serve as a blueprint for objects. Let's dive into the essentials of creating and initializing a class, keeping it beginner-friendly.

Creating a class:

To create a class, use the `class` keyword followed by the class name. Remember, class names conventionally start with a capital letter. Within the class, you can define attributes and methods.

Program code:
```
class MyClass:
    # Class attributes and methods go here
    pass
```

Initializing a class (constructor):

Initialization is crucial for setting up object attributes when an instance of the class is created. The `__init__` method acts as the constructor. Let's illustrate this with an example:

Program code:
```
class Dog:
    def __init__(self, name, age):
        self.name = name
        self.age = age

# Creating an instance of the Dog class
my_dog = Dog("Buddy", 3)

# Accessing attributes
print(my_dog.name)
print(my_dog.age)
```

Output:
```
Buddy
3
```

What to pay attention to:
- The `**self**` parameter in the `**__init__**` method refers to the instance of the class. It's a convention to use `**self**` but you can choose any name.
- When creating an instance of the class, Python automatically passes the instance as the first parameter to the `**__init__**` method.

What to remember:
- Class names begin with a capital letter.
- The `**__init__**` method initializes object attributes.

Useful tips:
- Meaningful attribute names enhance code readability.
- Initialize all necessary attributes in the `**__init__**` method.

108. Describe inheritance and its types in Python

In Python, inheritance is a powerful concept that allows a class to inherit properties and behaviors from another class. This promotes code reusability and helps create a logical hierarchy in your code. Let's dive into the essentials of inheritance with practical examples and key tips.

Types of inheritance:

Single inheritance

A class inherits from only one base class.

Program code:
```
class Animal:
    def speak(self):
        print("Animal speaks")
```

```
class Dog(Animal):
    def bark(self):
        print("Dog barks")


# Dog inherits from Animal
my_dog = Dog()
my_dog.speak()
my_dog.bark()
```

Output:

```
Animal speaks
Dog barks
```

Useful tip:

- Keep the hierarchy simple for better code understanding.

Multiple inheritance

A class can inherit from multiple base classes.

Program code:

```
class Flyable:
    def fly(self):
        print("Can fly")


class Swimmable:
    def swim(self):
        print("Can swim")


class FlyingFish(Flyable, Swimmable):
    pass


# FlyingFish inherits from Flyable and Swimmable
my_fish = FlyingFish()
my_fish.fly()
my_fish.swim()
```

Output:

```
Can fly
Can swim
```

Useful tip:

- Be cautious to avoid conflicts when using multiple inheritance.

Multilevel inheritance

A class inherits from another class, creating a chain of inheritance.

Program code:

```
class Vehicle:
    def start_engine(self):
        print("Engine started")


class Car(Vehicle):
    def drive(self):
        print("Car is moving")


class SportsCar(Car):
    def race(self):
        print("Sports car racing")


# SportsCar inherits from Car, which inherits from Vehicle
my_sports_car = SportsCar()
my_sports_car.start_engine()
my_sports_car.drive()
my_sports_car.race()
```

Output:

```
Engine started
Car is moving
Sports car racing
```

Useful tip:

- Keep the inheritance chain reasonable to maintain code simplicity.

What to remember:

- Code Reusability: Inheritance enables reuse of code, reducing redundancy.
- Method Overriding: Child classes can override methods of the parent class.
- Avoid Diamond Problem: Be cautious with multiple inheritance to prevent conflicts.

109. What is method overriding, and how is it implemented in Python?

In Python, method overriding allows you to redefine a method in a subclass that is already defined in its superclass. This feature empowers you to tailor the behavior of inherited methods to suit the specific needs of your subclass. Let's dive into the key aspects and practical implementation of method overriding.

What to pay attention to:

- Inheritance is Key: Method overriding is closely tied to the concept of inheritance. Ensure that your subclass inherits from the superclass containing the method you want to override.

How to implement method overriding:

Identical Signature: The overriding method in the subclass must have the same method signature (name and parameters) as the method in the superclass. This ensures a seamless replacement of the inherited method.

Use the 'super()' function: Inside the overriding method, you can use the `**super()**` function to call the method from the superclass. This helps maintain and extend the functionality of the overridden method.

Program code:

```
class Shape:
    def draw(self):
        print("Drawing a generic shape")

class Circle(Shape):
    def draw(self):
        super().draw()  # Calling the draw method from the superclass
        print("Drawing a circle")
```

```
# Creating instances
generic_shape = Shape()
custom_circle = Circle()

# Method calls
generic_shape.draw() # Output: Drawing a generic shape
custom_circle.draw() # Output: Drawing a generic shape\nDrawing a circle
```

Output:

```
Drawing a generic shape
Drawing a generic shape\nDrawing a circle
```

Useful tips:

- Enhance, Don't Replace: When overriding, aim to enhance the functionality of the inherited method rather than completely replacing it. This ensures that the core behavior is retained.
- Clear Documentation: Document the overridden methods to maintain code clarity for yourself and other developers.

What to remember:

- Dynamic Binding: Method overriding in Python involves dynamic binding, meaning the method to be called is determined during runtime based on the object type.

110. What is a `Class` in Python?

In Python, a `**class**` is a blueprint or a template for creating objects. It is a way to bundle data and functionality together.

Here are some key concepts related to classes in Python:

Object: An instance of a class. Objects have member variables and have behavior associated with them.

Attributes: Variables that store data, also known as fields or properties.

Methods: Functions that are associated with an object. They define the behavior of the class.

Constructor: A special method called when an object is created. It initializes the object's attributes.

111. How do you create an empty class in Python?

Creating an empty class in Python is as simple as it gets! You can define an empty class using the `**class**` keyword followed by the class name and a colon. Here's how you do it:

Program code:

```
class MyEmptyClass:
    pass
```

That's it! You've just created an empty class. You can think of a class as a blueprint for creating objects, and even though this class doesn't have any attributes or methods, you can always add them later when you need to.

What to remember:

- Python classes are incredibly flexible, and you can build on this foundation to create more complex classes with attributes and methods.

Program code:

```
class Car:
    def __init__(self, make, model, year):
        self.make = make
        self.model = model
        self.year = year

    def display_info(self):
        print(f"{self.year} {self.make} {self.model}")

# Creating an instance (object) of the Car class
my_car = Car("Toyota", "Camry", 2022)

# Accessing attributes
print(my_car.make)  # Output: Toyota

# Calling a method
my_car.display_info()  # Output: 2022 Toyota Camry
```

In this example, `**Car**` is a class with attributes (`**make**`, `**model**`, `**year**`) and a method (`**display_info**`). The `**__init__**` method is a special method that is called when an object is created, allowing you to set up the initial state of the object.

Classes provide a way to structure and organize code, and they are a fundamental concept in object-oriented programming (OOP). OOP allows you to model real-world entities and their interactions in a more natural and intuitive way.

112. What is `__init__` in Python?

In the realm of Python programming, the `**__init__**` method holds significant importance. This method, often referred to as a constructor in Object-Oriented Programming (OOP), serves as a pivotal building block for creating objects from a class.

At its core, the `**__init__**` method acts as a reserved function within Python. It gets invoked automatically when a new instance of a class is generated. Its primary purpose is to facilitate the initialization of the object's attributes and ensure that they are appropriately set up.

Think of the `**__init__**` method as the foundation upon which an object is constructed. When you create an object from a class, this method steps in to ensure that any initial data or attributes are established correctly. It's like the initial handshake between the object and the class blueprint.

To encapsulate, the `**__init__**` method's role in Python revolves around initializing the essential characteristics of an object and preparing it for use. This method underscores the fundamentals of Object-Oriented Programming by establishing a vital link between class definitions and actual object instances.

113. What is `self` in Python?

In Python, `**self**` is a special parameter that refers to the class instance. It allows a method to know which object it belongs to. When you define a method in a class, the instance that calls the method is passed automatically as the first parameter to the method. By convention, this parameter is named `**self**`, but you could name it anything you like, although it's recommended to stick with `**self**` for clarity.

Program code:

```
class MyClass:
def __init__(self, value):
    self.value = value

def display_value(self):
    print(self.value)

# Creating an instance of MyClass
obj = MyClass(42)

# Calling the display_value method
obj.display_value()
```

What to pay attention to:

- Always include `**self**` as the first parameter in the method definition within a class.
- Use `**self**` to access instance variables within the class.

Useful tip:

- Understanding `**self**` is fundamental to working with classes and objects in Python. It helps in differentiating instance variables from local variables within a class.

What to remember:

- `**self**` is a convention, not a keyword, and you could technically use any name you prefer, but it's best to stick with 'self' for clarity and consistency.

114. What is docstring in Python?

In Python, a docstring is like a friendly note attached to a function, method, class, or module. It's written within triple quotes and sits right after the definition. The main purpose of a docstring is to explain what that piece of code does. You can easily access these docstrings using the special `**__doc__**` attribute.

Here's a simple example to make things crystal clear:

Program code:

```
def square(n):
    '''Takes in a number n, returns the square of n'''
    return n**2
```

In this function, the docstring `**'''Takes in a number n, returns the square of n'''**` tells anyone reading your code that this function calculates the square of a number.

To see the docstring in action, you can do this:

Program code:

```
print(square.__doc__)
```

Output:

```
Takes in a number n, returns the square of n.
```

So, docstrings are like little helpers that make your code more understandable for you and anyone else reading it. They're a handy tool for keeping your codebase friendly and approachable.

115. How can an object be copied in Python?

In Python, duplicating an object is a common task, although it's worth noting that not all objects can be copied in the same way. The majority of objects, however, can be effectively copied. To achieve this, the assignment operator "=" can be employed, allowing the creation of a copy of an object within a new variable.

Program code:

```
import copy

# Creating a copy of an object
new_variable = copy.copy(original_object)
```

This technique utilizes the `**copy**` module to create a copy of the object stored in `**original_object**`, and then assigns it to the `**new_variable**`. While this method works well for many objects, it's essential to remember that certain objects might require more advanced copying techniques due to their complexity or reference structures.

116. Explaining modules and packages in Python

In Python, modules and packages are fundamental organizational tools that help structure and organize code in a logical and manageable way.

Modules:

A module is a single Python file that contains functions, classes, and variables. It acts as a container for reusable code. Modules can be created by creating a `**.py**` file with Python code. For example, if you have a file named `**my_module.py**` containing functions and variables, you can import and use them in other Python scripts by using the `import` statement:

```
import my_module
```

Modules facilitate code reusability and maintainability by allowing you to separate code into logical units.

Packages:

A package is a way of organizing related modules into a directory hierarchy. It can contain both modules and subpackages, forming a structured and organized codebase. Packages are created by organizing your Python files into directories and including a special `**__init__.py**` file in each directory to indicate that it's a package.

For example:

```
my_package/
 ├── __init__.py
 ├── module1.py
 └── module2.py
```

You can import modules from a package using dot notation:

```
import my_package.module1
```

Modules and packages offer several benefits:

- **Code organization:** Modules and packages provide a systematic way to organize your code, making it easier to navigate and understand large projects.

- **Encapsulation:** You can encapsulate related code in modules and packages, limiting the scope and making code more modular.

- **Reusability:** Modules promote code reuse since you can import and use functions and classes from different modules in various parts of your program.

- **Namespace management:** Modules and packages help in avoiding naming conflicts by creating separate namespaces for different components.

117. What is encapsulation?

Encapsulation in Python is like bundling up related code and data into a neat package, just like putting all your clothes into a suitcase before a trip. It's a way to keep things organized and prevent them from getting tangled up.

Think of a class in Python as a container. Inside this container, you put both data (attributes or variables) and the functions (methods) that work with that data. This way, you ensure that the data is protected and can only be accessed or modified in a controlled manner. For instance, let's create a simple class to encapsulate a person's information:

Program code:

```
class Person:
    def __init__(self, name, age):
        self.name = name
        self.age = age

    def greet(self):
        print(f"Hello, my name is {self.name} and I am {self.age} years old.")

# Creating an instance of the Person class
person1 = Person("Alice", 30)
```

Program code:

```
# Accessing data using encapsulation
print(person1.name)
```

Output:

```
Alice
```

Program code:

```
# Calling a method using encapsulation
person1.greet()
```

Output:

```
Hello, my name is Alice and I am 30 years old.
```

Here, the `**Person**` class encapsulates the `**name**` and `**age**` data along with the `**greet**` method to interact with that data. This prevents accidental or unauthorized access to the data, keeping it safe and organized.

Python Unit Testing

118. What is unittest in Python?

In Python, `unittest` is a built-in module that helps you write and run tests for your code. It's a vital tool for ensuring that your programs work as expected. With `unittest`, you can create test cases to check if your functions and classes perform correctly.

Let's say you have a function that adds two numbers:

Program code:

```
def add(a, b):
    return a + b
```

You can use `unittest` to test it:

Program code:

```
import unittest

class TestAddition(unittest.TestCase):
    def test_add_positive_numbers(self):
        self.assertEqual(add(3, 5), 8)  # Check if 3 + 5 equals 8

    def test_add_negative_numbers(self):
        self.assertEqual(add(-2, -4), -6)  # Check if -2 + (-4) equals -6

if __name__ == '__main__':
    unittest.main()
```

Useful tips:

- Test your code as you write it to catch bugs early.
- Maintain good test coverage to ensure all aspects of your code are tested.
- Make your test case names descriptive for clarity.

What to remember:

- `**unittest**` helps you find and fix issues in your code by automating the testing process.
- Test cases are like mini-programs that verify your code's correctness.
- Organize your tests into test suites to group related test cases.

`**unittest**` is a fantastic tool to boost your code's reliability and ensure that it behaves as expected.

119. Understanding the assert keyword in Python unittest

The "assert" keyword in Python unittest is a powerful tool for testing and debugging your code. It helps you ensure that certain conditions hold true during the execution of your program. Let's break down its usage and key points to keep in mind.

Usage and syntax:

```
assert expression, message
```

Here, "expression" is the condition you want to test, and "message" is an optional parameter that provides additional information about the assertion.

Program code:

```
def divide(a, b):
    assert b != 0, "Cannot divide by zero!"
    return a / b

result = divide(10, 2)
print(result)
```

Output:

```
5.0
```

In this example, the assert statement checks if the divisor (b) is not zero before performing the division. If the condition is false, it raises an AssertionError with the specified message.

What to pay attention to:

- Expression Evaluation: The expression after "assert" should evaluate to True for the program to continue execution.
- Error Handling: If the condition is False, an AssertionError is raised. Handle these exceptions appropriately in your code.

What to remember:

- Debugging Aid: Use assert statements to catch issues early in development.
- Keep it Simple: Asserts are meant for simple sanity checks, not complex logic.

Useful tips:

- Informative Messages: Include meaningful messages in assertions for better error identification.
- Enable/Disable: You can disable all assert statements globally with the `**-O**` (optimize) Python command line switch.

For beginners:

If you're new to Python, think of "assert" as your code's self-check mechanism. It ensures that your assumptions about your code remain true during its execution.

Remember, assert is a handy tool, but it's not a substitute for proper testing practices. As you progress in your Python learning, explore more about testing frameworks and best practices.

120. Creating a new test suite with Python unittest

Have you ever wondered how to set up a new test suite using Python's unittest module? It's simpler than you might think. Let's break it down:

Step 1: subclass unittest.TestSuite

To begin, subclass `**unittest.TestSuite**`. This allows you to create a custom test suite tailored to your needs. Here's a basic example:

Program code:

```
import unittest

class MyTestSuite(unittest.TestSuite):
    pass
```

Step 2: add your test cases

Now that you have your custom test suite, it's time to populate it with your test cases. Test cases are individual units of testing within your suite. Add them using the `**addTest**` method:

Program code:

```
class MyTestCase1(unittest.TestCase):
    def test_example(self):
        # Your test code here
        self.assertTrue(True)

class MyTestCase2(unittest.TestCase):
    def test_another_example(self):
        # More test code
        self.assertEqual(1 + 1, 2)

# Add your test cases to the suite
my_suite = MyTestSuite()
my_suite.addTest(MyTestCase1('test_example'))
my_suite.addTest(MyTestCase2('test_another_example'))
```

What to pay attention to:

- Ensure that your test cases cover various scenarios.
- Keep your test suite well-organized for easy maintenance.

Useful tips:

- Group-related tests in the same test case class.
- Name your test methods descriptively for clarity.

What to remember:

- Subclass `**unittest.TestSuite**` to create your suite.
- Use `**addTest**` to include your test cases in the suite.

121. What are some of the most commonly used assertion methods available for use in Python unittest?

Some of the most commonly used assertion methods in Python unittest are assertEqual(), assertTrue(), and assertFalse().

Let's dive into a few key ones with practical examples:

1. assertEqual(): This method is handy when you need to check if two values are equal. For instance:

Program code:
```
result = add_numbers(2, 3)
self.assertEqual(result, 5, "Adding 2 and 3 should equal 5")
```

What to remember:
- Use `**assertEqual()**` for comparing values.

2. assertTrue() and assertFalse(): These methods help verify whether a given condition is true or false, respectively. Consider the following:

Program code:
```
user_authenticated = check_user_authentication(user)
self.assertTrue(user_authenticated, "User should be authenticated")
```

What to remember:
- `**assertTrue()**` and `**assertFalse()**` are your go-to for checking conditions.

While more assertion methods are available, keeping these basics in mind will serve you well in interviews. Pay attention to the specific use cases of each method, and always include descriptive messages for better error identification.

Useful tip:
- Practice writing test cases using these assertion methods to strengthen your understanding. This not only helps in interviews but also enhances your overall coding skills.

122. How does one use multiple assertions to verify that all conditions have been met in Python unittest?

In Python unittests, ensuring that various conditions are met is crucial. Let's explore how to use the `**assertTrue()**` and `**assertFalse()**` methods to verify multiple conditions in a single test. This is not only efficient but also a fundamental skill for writing robust test cases.

Consider a scenario where you want to confirm that a list is not only non-empty but also has a first element greater than 5. You can achieve this with the following code snippet:

Program code:
```
assertTrue(len(mylist) > 0)
assertTrue(mylist[0] > 5)
```

What to pay attention to:

- **assertTrue() and assertFalse():** These methods play a key role in validating conditions. Use `**assertTrue()**` when the condition should be true and `**assertFalse()**` when it should be false.

Useful tip:

- **Informative assertions:** Craft assertions that provide clear failure messages. This aids in quickly identifying the cause of a test failure.

What to remember:

- **Single test, multiple conditions:** By chaining assertions, you can check several conditions in one go, making your tests concise and readable.
- **Order matters:** Be mindful of the order of your assertions. If the first one fails, the subsequent ones may not execute.

123. How to run your Python tests efficiently?

Ensuring your tests run swiftly and effectively is crucial for a smooth development process. Here are some practical tips and tools to optimize your Python tests, especially beneficial for beginners:

Utilize pytest for parallel execution:

Consider employing pytest, a powerful testing framework for Python. One standout feature is its ability to run tests in parallel, significantly boosting speed. To implement parallel execution with pytest, use the `**-n**` flag followed by the number of cores you want to utilize. For instance:

Program code:

```
pytest -n 4  # Runs tests across 4 cores
```

This approach is particularly useful when dealing with a large test suite, making the most of your computer's resources.

Leverage unittest's parallel features:

If you prefer using Python's built-in `**unittest**` module, fear not; it offers features for parallel test execution as well. You can achieve this by using the `**TestLoader**` class and the `**discover**` method. Here's a basic example:

Program code:

```
import unittest

class MyTests(unittest.TestCase):
   # Your test methods go here

if __name__ == '__main__':
   unittest.TextTestRunner().run(unittest.TestLoader().discover())
```

This simple script discovers and runs all tests in parallel, improving efficiency.

Minimize test dependencies:

Another key strategy is structuring your tests to reduce dependencies between them. When tests are independent, they can run concurrently without waiting for others to finish. This not only accelerates the testing process but also enhances test reliability.

Program code:

```
def test_addition():
   assert add(2, 3) == 5

def test_subtraction():
   assert subtract(5, 3) == 2
```

In this scenario, the `**test_addition**` and `**test_subtraction**` functions are independent, allowing them to run simultaneously without conflicts.

Useful tips:

- Aim for modular and focused tests.
- Regularly review and update your test suite for optimal performance.
- Explore additional testing tools and frameworks based on your project needs.

124. The significance of setup and teardown methods in unit testing

In the realm of unit testing, the use of setup and teardown methods is crucial for ensuring the reliability and consistency of your tests. Let's break down why these methods are essential for a seamless testing experience.

Why setup?

Imagine preparing a canvas before you start painting - that's what setup does for your unit tests. This method allows you to initialize the environment specifically tailored to each test. By doing so, you create a clean slate, ensuring that the conditions are just right for your test to run successfully.

Program code:

```
def setUp(self):
    # Initialize necessary resources or variables
    self.example_data = [1, 2, 3]

def test_sum_values(self):
    result = sum(self.example_data)
    self.assertEqual(result, 6)
```

What to pay attention to:

- Use setup to set the stage for your test by defining variables or resources needed.
- Keep it focused on the necessities of the specific test to avoid unnecessary clutter.

Why teardown?

Just as you clean up your painting supplies after creating a masterpiece, teardown is about tidying up after each test. This step ensures that no changes made during one test linger and affect the outcome of subsequent tests. It's all about maintaining a fresh start for each scenario.

Program code:

```
def tearDown(self):
    # Clean up resources or perform necessary actions
    self.example_data = None
```

Useful tips:

- Balance setup and teardown to strike a harmony between a well-prepared environment and a tidy aftermath.
- Keep each method concise and purpose-driven for maintainability.
- Think of setup and teardown as the opening and closing acts for your testing performance, ensuring a consistent and reliable show every time.

What to remember:

- Teardown is your chance to reset or release any resources acquired during the test.
- Keep it efficient, focusing on what needs to be cleaned up to avoid unnecessary overhead.

125. Is there any difference between `setUpClass()` and `tearDownClass()`?

`setUpClass()`

This nifty method kicks in at the start of your test suite, but just once. Need to establish a connection to a database, load some essential data, or prepare a common environment for your tests? This is the place to do it! Here's a quick example:

Program code:

```
import unittest

class MyTestClass(unittest.TestCase):

    @classmethod
    def setUpClass(cls):
        print("Setting up the class!")

        # Your setup code goes here
        # Connect to a database, load data, etc.

    def test_example(self):
        # Your test code goes here
        pass
```

`tearDownClass()`

Now, imagine `**tearDownClass()**` as the grand finale—it runs just once at the end of your test suite. This is where you tidy up everything, ensuring a clean slate after all the tests. If you opened a file, established a connection, or did anything in `**setUpClass()**`, this is your chance to close, disconnect, or undo it.

Program code:

```
import unittest

class MyTestClass(unittest.TestCase):

    @classmethod
    def setUpClass(cls):
        print("Setting up the class!")

    @classmethod
    def tearDownClass(cls):
        print("Tearing down the class!")

        # Your teardown code goes here
        # Close files, disconnect from a database, etc.

    def test_example(self):
        # Your test code goes here
        pass
```

Useful tip:

- Whatever you set up in `**setUpClass()**`, make sure to clean it up in `**tearDownClass()**` to keep things neat and tidy.

126. How can you skip a particular test method or class using the decorator @unittest.skip?

Skipping a specific test method or class in Python is made easy with the @unittest.skip decorator. This handy tool allows you to temporarily disable tests or skip them when you anticipate compatibility issues with your system.

Program code:

```
import unittest

class MyTestCase(unittest.TestCase):

    @unittest.skip("Reason for skipping")
    def test_skip_this_method(self):
        # Your test code here

    @unittest.skipIf(condition, "Reason for skipping if condition is True")
    def test_skip_if_condition_true(self):
        # Your test code here

    @unittest.skipUnless(condition, "Reason for skipping unless condition is
True")
    def test_skip_unless_condition_true(self):
        # Your test code here
```

What to pay attention to:

- Provide a clear reason for skipping using the decorator argument.
- Use `**@unittest.skipIf**` to skip based on a specific condition.
- Utilize `**@unittest.skipUnless**` when skipping unless a condition is met.

Useful tips:

- Use the decorator judiciously, and document the reason for skipping to maintain code transparency.
- Regularly review and update skipped tests to ensure they align with the current system environment.

What to remember:

- This is handy for temporarily disabling tests or handling system-specific issues.
- Keep your tests up to date, revisiting skipped tests when system conditions change.

Skipping tests is a useful strategy for managing your test suite effectively and ensuring that your test suite runs smoothly across different environments.

127. What is the difference between the `assertTrue()` and `assertFalse()` methods?

In Python, the `**assertTrue()**` and `**assertFalse()**` methods play a crucial role in verifying conditions within your code. Let's break down their differences and see how they can be applied in practical scenarios.

1. `assertTrue()` method:

This method comes into play when you want to ensure that a specific condition evaluates to `**True**`. Imagine you have a function that should always return a positive result. You can use `**assertTrue()**` to confirm this:

Program code:

```
# Example: Ensuring a function returns a positive result
result = some_function()
assertTrue(result > 0, "The result should be positive.")
```

What to pay attention to:

- Make sure to provide a clear message as the second argument. This helps in identifying issues when the condition is not met.
- Use this method when validating positive outcomes in your code.

2. `assertFalse()` method:

Contrastingly, the `**assertFalse()**` method checks if a condition is `**False**`. Consider a situation where you want to confirm that a variable is not empty:

Program code:

```
# Example: Verifying a variable is not empty
my_variable = some_operation()
assertFalse(not my_variable, "The variable should not be empty.")
```

Useful tips:

- These methods are handy in unit testing to validate the correctness of your functions.
- Always pair them with meaningful messages to quickly identify issues.

What to remember:

- Similar to `**assertTrue()**`, include a descriptive message for better troubleshooting.
- Employ `**assertFalse()**` when you need to validate negative conditions.

In summary, `**assertTrue()**` and `**assertFalse()**` are valuable tools for validating conditions in your Python code. Whether you're confirming positive outcomes or ensuring certain conditions are not met, these methods contribute to writing robust and error-resistant programs.

128. What is the purpose of the `assertNotEquals()` method?

The assertNotEquals() method serves the purpose of verifying that two values are not equal. Unlike the assertEquals() method, which confirms equality, assertNotEquals() is designed to ensure inequality between two values.

Program code:

```
# Example usage of assertNotEquals()
value1 = 10
value2 = 20

assertNotEquals(value1, value2, "Values should not be equal")
```

What to pay attention to:

Ensure that the two values being compared are genuinely different. This method is handy for validating distinctions between variables.

Useful tip:

- Consider using assertNotEquals() when comparing variables in unit tests or scenarios where inequality is crucial for correct program behavior.

What to remember:

- Use assertNotEquals() when you expect two values to be different.
- Always provide a meaningful message to enhance clarity in case of failure.

129. What do you think is the biggest problem with unit tests?

One notable challenge in unit testing revolves around the investment of time required for both creation and upkeep. Ensuring that your test suite stays relevant as your code evolves is crucial to avoid misleading results—either false positives or false negatives. While maintaining tests demands effort, it's a necessary aspect of effective coding. Let's delve into a few key considerations to address this challenge:

What to pay attention to:

- Consistent Updates: Regularly update your tests to align with changes in your codebase. This prevents inaccuracies that may arise due to outdated tests.
- Review Dependencies: Check for dependencies between tests and your code. Changes in one area might affect others, leading to potential discrepancies.

Useful tips:

- Test-Driven Development (TDD): Consider adopting TDD practices. Writing tests before implementing code encourages a systematic approach and helps in keeping tests and code in sync.
- Team Collaboration: Foster collaboration within your team for shared responsibility in maintaining tests. This can distribute the workload and ensure more comprehensive coverage.

What to remember:

- Test Quality Over Quantity: Focus on creating meaningful tests rather than a sheer volume. Well-designed tests are easier to maintain and provide more accurate insights into your code's functionality.
- Automation is Your Friend: Leverage automation tools to streamline the testing process. Automated testing not only saves time but also reduces the chances of overlooking updates.

Maintaining unit tests might seem daunting initially, but it's an investment that pays off in the long run. Strive for a balance between thorough testing and efficient maintenance, and you'll find that the benefits far outweigh the efforts.

Pandas and NumPy in Python

130. What are Pandas?

Pandas is an amazing open-source Python library that comes with a treasure trove of data structures tailor-made for all your data-related needs. Whether you're a student diving into academics or a professional tackling intricate business challenges, Pandas has got your back!

With its cool features and versatility, Pandas can handle a vast range of data files, making it an essential tool in your programming arsenal. It's like having a trusty sidekick that can process and manipulate data with ease.

No matter if you're dealing with CSVs, Excel spreadsheets, SQL databases, or even JSON files, Pandas can gracefully handle them all. Plus, its intuitive and user-friendly syntax makes working with data a breeze!

131. Explain the role of Pandas in Data Analysis

Pandas are like a data superhero for Python developers, making it easy to work with structured data. Its primary structures, the DataFrame and Series, empower you to handle, clean, and analyze data efficiently.

Let's say you have a dataset with information about sales. Using Pandas, you can load this data into a DataFrame, allowing you to explore, filter, and transform it effortlessly.

Program code:

```
import pandas as pd

# Reading data from a CSV file into a DataFrame
sales_data = pd.read_csv('sales_data.csv')

# Displaying the first few rows of the DataFrame
print(sales_data.head())
```

What to pay attention to:

- When working with Pandas, pay attention to your data's syntax and structure. Ensure that column names are clear and data types are appropriate. This attention to detail will save you from potential errors during analysis.

Useful tips:

- Use the `**describe()**` function to get statistical insights into your data quickly.
- Utilize the `**isnull()**` function to identify missing values in your dataset.
- Master the art of indexing and slicing to extract specific data portions.

What to remember:

- Remember that Pandas offer many functions for data manipulation, such as filtering, sorting, and aggregating. Familiarize yourself with these tools to unlock the full potential of your data.

Suitable for beginners:

- Pandas may seem overwhelming at first, but fear not! Start with simple tasks like loading data and displaying basic statistics. Gradually, you'll become comfortable with its vast capabilities.

132. What are DataFrames?

DataFrames are an essential part of Pandas, a powerful Python library for data manipulation and analysis. Imagine DataFrames as flexible containers that can hold all sorts of data, arranged neatly across rows and columns.

So, what exactly is a DataFrame? Well, think of it as a mutable data structure in Pandas. It's like a table where each row represents a unique record, and each column corresponds to a specific data attribute.

For example, let's say we have a CSV file called `**mydata.csv**` containing some information we want to analyze. To load this data into Pandas and create a data frame, we use a simple method:

Program Code:

```
import pandas as pd
df = pd.read_csv("mydata.csv")
```

Here, pd is just an alias for Pandas, making it easier to work with. The `**read_csv()**` function does the magic of reading the contents of the CSV file and transforming it into a DataFrame named `**df**`.

Now, you have all the data from the CSV file neatly organized into a Pandas DataFrame, ready for analysis and manipulation. You can perform various operations like filtering, grouping, and calculations on this DataFrame to derive valuable insights and answers to your questions.

133. How can you create a 5x5 NumPy array filled with zeroes?

To initialize a 5x5 NumPy array with only zeroes, we can use the `**.zeros()**` method. First, make sure to import the NumPy library by adding `**import numpy as np**` at the beginning of your code.

Now, you can create the array by using the `**.zeros()**` method and passing the desired dimensions inside it. Since we want a 5x5 matrix, we'll use `**(5, 5)**` as the argument for `**.zeros()**`.

Here's the code snippet to achieve this:

```
import numpy as np
n1 = np.zeros((5, 5))
print(n1)
```

When you run this code, you will get a 5x5 NumPy array filled with zeroes.

This array will look like this:

```
[[0. 0. 0. 0. 0.]
 [0. 0. 0. 0. 0.]
 [0. 0. 0. 0. 0.]
 [0. 0. 0. 0. 0.]
 [0. 0. 0. 0. 0.]]
```

Using the `**.zeros()**` method makes it easy to create arrays of any desired dimensions filled with zeros, which is often useful in various data science and numerical computing tasks.

134. What is a Pandas Series?

Imagine a Pandas Series as a super useful one-dimensional data structure, kind of like an Excel column. It's like a container that can hold data of various types, be it numbers, text, or even a mix of both.

To create a Pandas Series, you'll first need to import the Pandas library using the line `**import pandas as pd**`. This library is a powerhouse for data manipulation and analysis.

Next, we can start building our Series. Let's say we have some data like ["1", 2, "three", 4.0]. We'll pass this data into the `**pd.Series()**` function, like this:

Program code:

```
import pandas as pd

data = ["1", 2, "three", 4.0]
series = pd.Series(data)
```

And voilà! You've just created a Pandas Series.

Now, if you want to see what's inside this Series, use the `**print(series)**` statement, and it will show you the data:

Output:

```
0    1
1    2
2    three
3    4.0
```

Looks nice, right? The Series has neatly organized our data, showing each element along with its index. Python will automatically assign a numerical index to each item in the Series.

Oh, and one more thing! If you're curious about the data type of the Series itself, use `**print(type(series))**`, and Python will tell you that it's a Pandas Series.

135. What do you understand about Pandas `groupby()`?

Pandas `**groupby()**` is an incredibly useful feature supported by the Pandas library in Python. It allows us to split and group data into subsets based on a specific criterion. Think of it like the `**GROUP BY**` clause in SQL or similar concepts in MySQL or Oracle databases. With Pandas groupby, we can organize our data by classes, categories, or entities, which can then be used for various aggregations and analyses.

Let's understand this with a simple example. Suppose we have a DataFrame containing information about vehicles and their types:

Program code:

```
import pandas as pd

df = pd.DataFrame({'Vehicle': ['Etios', 'Lamborghini', 'Apache200',
'Pulsar200'],
             'Type': ['car', 'car', 'motorcycle', 'motorcycle']})

print(df)
```

This will give us the following DataFrame:

```
        Vehicle              Type
0       Etios                car
1       Lamborghinicar
2       Apache200            motorcycle
3       Pulsar200            motorcycle
```

Now, to perform a `**groupby()**` based on the `**Type**` column, we use the following code:

Program code:

```
grouped_df = df.groupby('Type').count()
print(grouped_df)
```

This will output:

```
            Vehicle
Type
Car         2
motorcycle  2
```

As you can see, the DataFrame has been grouped based on the `**Type**` column, and Pandas counted the occurrences of each type. In this case, we have two cars and two motorcycles in our data.

Pandas `**groupby()**` is a powerful tool that allows us to split, apply operations, and combine data efficiently. It's commonly used in data analysis and data preprocessing tasks, making it a crucial concept to understand for any Python developer working with data.

136. How to create a DataFrame from lists?

Creating a DataFrame from lists is a common task in Python, especially when dealing with data analysis and manipulation. Let's walk through the steps:

Step 1: First, we need to create an empty DataFrame. We'll use the Pandas library, so make sure you have it installed and imported in your Python environment.

Program code:

```
import pandas as pd
df = pd.DataFrame()
```

Step 2: Now, we'll prepare our lists. For this example, we have two lists - one for cars and another for bikes. Feel free to use your own lists or modify these as per your data.

Program code:

```
bikes = ["bajaj", "tvs", "herohonda", "kawasaki", "bmw"]
cars = ["lamborghini", "maserati", "ferrari", "hyundai", "ford"]
```

Step 3: The final step is to add these lists as individual columns to our DataFrame. We do this by simply assigning the lists to the DataFrame using square brackets.

Program code:

```
df["cars"] = cars
df["bikes"] = bikes
```

Step 4: To see the result, just print the DataFrame.

Program code:

```
print(df)
```

And there you have it! You've successfully created a DataFrame from lists. The output will show the `**cars**` and `**bikes**` lists as two separate columns, forming a tabular representation of the data.

Output:

```
    cars          bikes
0   lamborghini   bajaj
1   maserati      tvs
2   ferrari       herohonda
3   hyundai       kawasaki
4   ford          bmw
```

137. How to create a DataFrame from a dictionary?

Creating a data frame from a dictionary in Python is quite straightforward. You can achieve this by directly passing the dictionary as an argument to the `**DataFrame()**` function provided by the Pandas library.

Here's an example code snippet:

Program code:

```
import pandas as pd

bikes = ["bajaj", "tvs", "herohonda", "kawasaki", "bmw"]
cars = ["lamborghini", "masserati", "ferrari", "hyundai", "ford"]
d = {"cars": cars, "bikes": bikes}

df = pd.DataFrame(d)
print(df)
```

In this code, we first import the Pandas library as `**pd**`, which is a popular library for data manipulation and analysis. Then, we define two lists, `**bikes**` and `**cars**`, containing some sample data.

Next, we create a dictionary `**d**` with keys `**cars**` and `**bikes**` and their corresponding lists as values. The next step is the crucial part — we pass this dictionary `**d**` as an argument to `**pd.DataFrame()**` to create the data frame `**df**`.

When you run this code, you'll see the resulting data frame that neatly organizes the data from the dictionary into rows and columns:

Output:

```
    cars          bikes
0   lamborghini   bajaj
1   masserati     tvs
2   ferrari       herohonda
3   hyundai       kawasaki
4   ford          bmw
```

138. How to combine DataFrames in Pandas?

In Pandas, you can effortlessly combine two different DataFrames, either horizontally or vertically, using the powerful functions concat(), append(), and join(). These functions make data manipulation a breeze and can be your go-to tools for merging DataFrames effectively.

concat()

The `**concat()**` function is perfect for vertically stacking DataFrames that share the same columns. It's like combining multiple DataFrames into a single, unified DataFrame. So, if you have data with similar fields, this is the way to go!

append()

Need to horizontally stack DataFrames? `**Append()**` has got your back! When you have two tables (DataFrames) that you want to merge side by side, this function is your best friend. It helps you effortlessly join data horizontally.

join()

Imagine you have different DataFrames with one or more common columns, and you want to extract specific data from them. The join function is the answer! It performs a horizontal stacking of data based on those common columns.

139. What kind of joins does Pandas offer?

Pandas is awesome when it comes to data manipulation, and it offers four types of joins to merge datasets seamlessly. Here they are:

Left join

This join keeps all the rows from the left DataFrame and combines them with matching rows from the right DataFrame. If there's no match, it fills in with NaN values.

Inner join

The inner join only returns the rows that have matching keys in both DataFrames. It discards non-matching rows from both sides.

Right join

Similar to the left join, but this one keeps all the rows from the right DataFrame and combines them with matching rows from the left DataFrame. Non-matching rows are filled with NaN values.

Outer join

The outer join combines all rows from both DataFrames, filling in with NaN values when there are no matches.

When you're dealing with multiple datasets, knowing the right type of join can make your data analysis a breeze!

140. How to merge DataFrames in Pandas?

Well, merging DataFrames can be super useful when you want to combine data from different sources. Let me break it down for you!

When you merge DataFrames in Pandas, the approach you take depends on the type and fields of the DataFrames you're dealing with. If both DataFrames have similar fields, Pandas will merge the data along what we call "axis 0" (which is the rows). This is great when you have data that you want to stack on top of each other.

On the other hand, if the DataFrames have different fields, Pandas will merge them along "axis 1" (which is the columns). This is handy when you want to add new columns to your existing DataFrame with additional information.

So, whether you're looking to stack your data or add more columns, Pandas has got you covered when it comes to merging DataFrames.

141. Give the below DataFrame drop all rows having `NaN`

To remove all rows containing `**NaN**` values from a DataFrame, you can use the `**dropna()**` function. This function allows you to clean up your data effectively. Here's how you can do it:

Program code:

```
# Assuming 'df' is your DataFrame
df.dropna(inplace=True)
```

By setting `**inplace=True**`, the DataFrame will be modified in place, meaning the rows with `**NaN**` will be removed, and the changes will be applied directly to the original DataFrame.

Make sure to use this method when you want to clean your data and eliminate any rows with missing values, so your analysis or machine learning models can work smoothly without any issues.

142. How to access the first five entries of a DataFrame?

You can use the `**head(5)**` function to get the first five entries of your DataFrame. By default, when you call `**df.head()**`, it will return the top 5 rows. But if you want more or fewer rows, you can simply specify the number you need, like `**df.head(10)**` to get the top ten rows. It's a handy trick to quickly peek at the beginning of your data and get a sense of what's there!

143. How to access the last five entries of a DataFrame?

To access the last five entries of a DataFrame in Python, you can use the `**tail(5)**` function. It's a handy method that automatically gives you the last five rows of the DataFrame by default. But, if you specifically want the last '**n**' rows, you can pass the desired value to the `**tail()**` function, like `**df.tail(n)**`.

So, whether you need just the most recent records or want to see more than five rows from the end, `**tail()**` has got you covered! It's a useful tool when you're dealing with large datasets and want to quickly check the latest data points in your DataFrame.

144. How to fetch a data entry from a Pandas DataFrame using a given value in index?

To fetch a specific row from a Pandas DataFrame based on a given index value, you can utilize the `**loc**` method.

In the example below, we have a DataFrame containing information about cars and bikes. Let's see how to retrieve the row with an index value of 10:

Program code:

```
import pandas as pd

bikes = ["bajaj", "tvs", "herohonda", "kawasaki", "bmw"]
cars = ["lamborghini", "masserati", "ferrari", "hyundai", "ford"]
data = {"cars": cars, "bikes": bikes}
df = pd.DataFrame(data)

# Assigning custom index values
custom_index = [10, 20, 30, 40, 50]
df.index = custom_index

# Fetching the row with index value 10 using loc
result_row = df.loc[20]
print(result_row)
```

Output:

```
cars        masserati
bikes       tvs
Name: 20,   dtype: object
```

The `**loc**` method allows us to access rows based on their index label, which, in this case, is the value 20. When we run the code, it will display the row that corresponds to the index value of 20.

By using `**loc**`, you can easily retrieve specific data entries from your Pandas DataFrame.

145. How to create a new column in Pandas using values from other columns?

In Pandas, creating new columns by performing mathematical operations on existing ones is easy. Let's see how you can do this with a simple example. We'll create a DataFrame and add two new columns that represent the sum and difference of values from existing columns.

Step 1: Import Pandas

First, you need to import the Pandas library. This allows you to work with DataFrames and perform various data manipulation tasks.

Program code:

```
import pandas as pd
```

Step 2: Create a DataFrame

Next, you can create a DataFrame with two columns, `**col1**` and `**col2**`, which contain some numeric values.

Program code:

```
a = [1, 2, 3]
b = [2, 3, 5]
data = {"col1": a, "col2": b}
df = pd.DataFrame(data)
```

Your DataFrame 'df' now looks like this:

```
     col1  col2
0    1     2
1    2     3
2    3     5
```

Step 3: Create new columns

Now, let's create two new columns, `**Sum**` and `**Difference**`, by adding and subtracting the values from `**col1**` and `**col2**`, respectively.

Program code:

```
df["Sum"] = df["col1"] + df["col2"]
df["Difference"] = df["col1"] - df["col2"]
```

Step 4: Display the DataFrame

Finally, you can display the DataFrame to see the new columns you've added.

Program code:

```
print(df)
```

The output will be:

```
     col1  col2  Sum  Difference
0    1     2     3    -1
1    2     3     5    -1
2    3     5     8    -2
```

You've successfully created new columns in a Pandas DataFrame using values from other columns. You can use this technique to perform various operations on your data and make it more useful for analysis.

146. How can you use the `groupby()` function in Pandas?

And what practical aggregation functions can you apply?

In Pandas, the `**groupby()**` function is a handy tool for organizing and summarizing data. It allows you to group your data based on certain categories and then apply various aggregation functions to those groups. Here are a few practical examples of aggregation functions you can use with `**groupby()**`:

sum()
This function calculates the sum of values within each group. For instance, you can find the total sales per category.

mean()
It computes the average values in each group. An example might be determining the average score of students in different classes.

count()
This function counts the number of elements in each group. You could use it to count the number of data points in different categories.

std()
This calculates the standard deviation within each group. It's useful when you want to measure the variability within categories.

Let's say you have a sales dataset and want to find the total sales for each product category. You can use `**groupby()**` with the `**sum()**` function like this:

Program code:

```
import pandas as pd

# Create a DataFrame with your sales data
data = {
    'Product': ['A', 'B', 'A', 'B', 'A'],
    'Sales': [100, 150, 200, 75, 120]
}

df = pd.DataFrame(data)

# Group by 'Product' and calculate the total sales for each category
result = df.groupby('Product')['Sales'].sum()
print(result)
```

Output:

```
Product
A    420
B    225
Name: Sales, dtype: int64
```

This output shows the total sales for each product category (`**A**` and `**B**`) after using the `**groupby()**` function with the `**sum()**` aggregation function.

By using the `**groupby()**` function along with these aggregation functions, you can gain valuable insights from your data, even if you're just starting with Python and Pandas.

147. How to delete a column or group of columns in Pandas?

How to delete a single column?

Here's how you can remove a column named `**example_column**` from a DataFrame `**df**`:

Program code:

```
df.drop('example_column', axis=1, inplace=True)
```

* `**axis=1**` indicates we're removing a column (not a row).
* `**inplace=True**` ensures the changes are made directly to `**df**` without needing to assign it back.

How to delete multiple columns?
To remove a list of columns, like `**column1**`, `**column2**`, and `**column3**` from `**df**`:

Program code:
```
columns_to_remove = ['column1', 'column2', 'column3']
df.drop(columns=columns_to_remove, inplace=True)
```

What to remember:
- Use `**drop**` method to remove columns.
- Specify the columns to remove.
- Always set `**axis=1**` to indicate you're targeting columns.

Let's dive into a practical example. We'll first create a sample DataFrame and then show how to delete specific columns from it.

Imagine you have a DataFrame that contains data about students, including their names, ages, grades, and hobbies:

Program code:
```
import pandas as pd

data = {
   'Name': ['Alice', 'Bob', 'Charlie', 'David'],
   'Age': [24, 28, 22, 19],
   'Grade': ['A', 'B', 'A', 'C'],
   'Hobby': ['Reading', 'Cycling', 'Swimming', 'Singing']
}

df = pd.DataFrame(data)

print("Original DataFrame:")
print(df)
```

Output:
```
      Name      Age  Grade     Hobby
0     Alice     24   A         Reading
1     Bob       28   B         Cycling
2     Charlie   22   A         Swimming
3     David     19   C         Singing
```

Deleting a single column:

Let's say we don't need the 'Hobby' column anymore. Here's how you can remove it:

Program code:

```
df.drop('Hobby', axis=1, inplace=True)
print("\nDataFrame after dropping 'Hobby' column:")
print(df)
```

Output:

```
DataFrame after dropping 'Hobby' column:
      Name     Age  Grade
0     Alice    24   A
1     Bob      28   B
2     Charlie  22   A
3     David    19   C
```

Deleting multiple columns:

Now, if we also want to remove the 'Age' and 'Grade' columns:

Program code:

```
columns_to_remove = ['Age', 'Grade']
df.drop(columns=columns_to_remove, inplace=True)
print("\nDataFrame after dropping 'Age' and 'Grade' columns:")
print(df)
```

Output:

```
DataFrame after dropping 'Age' and 'Grade' columns:
 Name
0     Alice
1     Bob
2     Charlie
3     David
```

Whether you're removing one column or several, the `**drop**` method in Pandas makes it super easy.

148. Given the following DataFrame, drop rows having column values as A

You have a DataFrame (essentially a table of data) and you want to remove certain rows based on specific values in one of its columns.

Example: Let's say you have a DataFrame with two columns: `**col1**` containing numbers and `**col2**` containing letters. You'd like to remove any row where `**col2**` has the value `**A**`.

Here's the data you have:

```
d = {"col1": [1, 2, 3], "col2": ["A", "B", "C"]}
```

It looks something like this:

```
col1    col2
1       A
2       B
3       C
```

Now, you want to remove the rows where `**col2**` is `**A**`.

Step-by-step Code:

STEP 1. First, create the DataFrame:

```
import pandas as pd

d = {"col1": [1, 2, 3], "col2": ["A", "B", "C"]}
df = pd.DataFrame(d)
```

STEP 2. Drop any rows with missing values (though in this example, there aren't any):

```
df.dropna(inplace=True)
```

STEP 3. Remove rows where `col2` has the value `A`:

```
df = df[df.col2 != "A"]
```

Your DataFrame (`**df**`) will now look like this:

```
col1    col2
2       B
3       C
```

There you go! You've successfully filtered out rows based on specific column values in a DataFrame.

149. Reindexing in Pandas

Definition:

Reindexing in Pandas refers to the process of altering the index (row labels) and/or columns of a DataFrame or Series. This can be useful when you want to align data with a new set of labels or when you need to change the order of existing rows/columns.

Practical Example: Suppose you have a DataFrame of fruits with their corresponding prices:

Program code:

```
import pandas as pd

data = {'Fruits': ['Apple', 'Banana', 'Cherry'], 'Price': [1.2, 0.5, 2.5]}
df = pd.DataFrame(data)

print(df)
```

Output:

```
      Fruits     Price
0     Apple      1.2
1     Banana     0.5
2     Cherry     2.5
```

Now, you want to change the order of the fruits (rows) and perhaps include a fruit that's not there:

Program code:

```
new_order = [2, 0, 1, 3]
fruits_reindexed = df.reindex(new_order, fill_value={'Fruits': 'Orange',
'Price': 1.8})

print(fruits_reindexed)
```

Output:

```
      Fruits    Price
2     Cherry    2.5
0     Apple     1.2
1     Banana    0.5
3     Orange    1.8
```

As you can see, the rows are rearranged based on the new order, and the missing fruit, Orange, is added with a default price.

Useful tips:

- While reindexing, if you reference an index that doesn't exist in the original DataFrame, Pandas will introduce NaN values. Using `**fill_value**` helps provide default values for such cases.
- Reindexing can be handy when merging or combining data from different sources.

What to remember:

- Reindexing is about aligning data to a new set of labels.
- Always watch out for NaN values and handle them appropriately.
- It's handy when working with data from diverse sources or when you need to reorder rows/columns.

150. What is NumPy?

NumPy is a powerful numerical computing library for Python. It provides support for large, multi-dimensional arrays and matrices, along with a collection of mathematical functions to operate on these elements. NumPy is a fundamental package for scientific computing in Python, and it forms the foundation for various other libraries in the data science and machine learning ecosystem.

Key features of NumPy include:

Arrays: NumPy introduces the `**ndarray**` data type, which is an efficient, multidimensional array providing fast mathematical operations.

Mathematical Functions: NumPy includes a wide range of mathematical functions that operate on arrays, making it convenient for numerical operations and analysis.

Broadcasting: NumPy supports broadcasting, allowing operations on arrays of different shapes and sizes without the need for explicit loops.

Linear Algebra: NumPy provides a rich set of functions for linear algebra operations, including matrix multiplication, eigenvalue decomposition, and solving linear equations.

Random: It includes functions for generating random numbers and random sampling, essential for simulations and statistical analysis.

NumPy is a core library for numerical and scientific computing in Python and is widely used in fields such as data science, machine learning, signal processing, and more. Its efficient array operations and versatility make it a crucial tool for handling large datasets and performing complex mathematical computations.

151. Describe the significance of NumPy and how to use it

NumPy is a powerhouse for numerical operations in Python, empowering you to work efficiently with arrays and matrices. Let's dive into its significance and how to leverage its capabilities.

Why NumPy Matters:

NumPy, short for Numerical Python, is a fundamental library for scientific computing. It excels in handling large datasets and performing complex mathematical operations with ease. Here's why it's a game-changer:

1. Efficient Arrays: NumPy introduces the array, a versatile data structure that outperforms traditional lists, especially when dealing with numerical data.

2. Speed and Performance: NumPy is optimized for speed, making it the go-to choice for data-intensive tasks. Its underlying C implementation ensures rapid execution of operations.

3. Broad Application: From basic arithmetic to advanced mathematical functions, NumPy simplifies complex computations. It's widely used in fields like data science, machine learning, and engineering.

How to harness NumPy's power:

Let's get hands-on with NumPy! Here's a brief guide on using it effectively:

1. Installation: Ensure NumPy is installed using `**pip install numpy**` in your terminal or command prompt.

2. Importing NumPy: Start your script by importing NumPy:

Program code:
```
import numpy as np
```

The alias `**np**` is a convention widely adopted in the Python community.

3. Creating arrays:

Program code:
```
# 1D array
array_1d = np.array([1, 2, 3])

# 2D array (matrix)
array_2d = np.array([[1, 2, 3], [4, 5, 6]])
```

4. Array operations:

Program code:
```
# Element-wise addition
result = array_1d + 5

# Matrix multiplication
result_matrix = np.dot(array_2d, array_2d.T)
```

5. Universal functions (ufuncs):
NumPy provides a plethora of ufuncs for common operations:

Program code:
```
# Square root of an array
sqrt_array = np.sqrt(array_1d)
```

What to remember:

- Data Types: Be mindful of data types, as NumPy arrays are homogeneous. Specify types explicitly if needed.
- Broadcasting: NumPy's broadcasting rules enable operations on arrays of different shapes. Understand this feature for efficient code.
- Documentation: NumPy's documentation is a goldmine. Refer to it for in-depth exploration and understanding.

152. How do you create a NumPy array in Python?

Creating a NumPy array in Python is a fundamental skill. You can initiate an array using the `**numpy.array()**` function.

To create a NumPy array, follow these steps:

1. Import NumPy:
First, make sure to import the NumPy library. You can do this by adding the following line at the beginning of your script or notebook:

Program code:
```
import numpy as np
```

This allows you to use the shorthand "np" when referring to NumPy.

2. Use `numpy.array()`:
Now, utilize the `**numpy.array()**` function to create an array. You can pass a Python list or tuple as an argument:

Program code:
```
my_list = [1, 2, 3, 4, 5]
my_array = np.array(my_list)
```

Alternatively, you can directly pass a list to `**numpy.array()**`:

Program code:
```
my_array = np.array([1, 2, 3, 4, 5])
```

Let's say you want to create an array of zeros. NumPy provides the `**numpy.zeros()**` function for this purpose. Here's how you can use it:

Program code:
```
zero_array = np.zeros(5)
print(zero_array)
```

This creates a NumPy array filled with zeros, with the specified length of 5.

What to pay attention to:

- Ensure you have NumPy installed. If not, you can install it using `**pip install numpy**`.
- NumPy arrays are homogeneous, meaning they contain elements of the same data type.

Useful tips:

- Explore other NumPy functions like `**numpy.zeros()**`, `**numpy.ones()**`, and `**numpy.arange()**` for array initialization.
- Familiarize yourself with NumPy's array attributes, such as shape and dtype, for effective array manipulation.

What to remember:

- Import NumPy using `**import numpy as np**`.
- Use `**numpy.array()**` to create arrays from Python lists or tuples.

153. What are the advantages of using NumPy over Python Lists?

While Python Lists are versatile, NumPy arrays offer several advantages that make them a preferred choice in many scenarios.

1. Performance Boost:

NumPy arrays are more efficient than Python Lists when dealing with large datasets. This is due to NumPy's implementation in C, which leads to faster execution.

Program code:

```
# Python List
python_list = [1, 2, 3, 4, 5]

# NumPy Array
import numpy as np
numpy_array = np.array([1, 2, 3, 4, 5])
```

2. Unified Operations:

NumPy enables you to perform operations on entire arrays, eliminating the need for explicit loops. This results in cleaner and more concise code.

Program code:

```
# Adding two Python Lists
result_list = [a + b for a, b in zip(list1, list2)]

# Adding two NumPy Arrays
result_array = array1 + array2
```

What to pay attention to:

- **Data Types:** NumPy arrays are homogeneous, meaning all elements must be of the same data type. Be mindful of the data types you use to prevent unexpected behavior.

Program code:

```
# Specify data type in NumPy array
np_array = np.array([1, 2, 3], dtype=np.float64)
```

- **Memory Efficiency:** NumPy arrays consume less memory compared to Python Lists, especially when dealing with large datasets. This efficiency is crucial for performance optimization.

154. How can you reshape a NumPy array?

Reshaping a NumPy array is a handy skill that allows you to transform its dimensions to fit your specific needs. Let's explore how to do this effectively.

Program code:

```
import numpy as np

# Create a 1D array
original_array = np.array([1, 2, 3, 4, 5, 6])

# Reshape to a 2D array with 2 rows and 3 columns
reshaped_array = original_array.reshape(2, 3)

print(reshaped_array)
```

What to pay attention to:

- Compatible Dimensions: Ensure that the total number of elements in the original array is compatible with the new shape. The product of dimensions should be the same for both.

- Contiguous Data: Reshaping creates a view of the original array, but for some reshapes, a contiguous array may be required. In such cases, you can use `**np.copy()**` to create a new contiguous array.

Useful tips:

- Check the Shape: Always double-check the shape of the reshaped array using the `**shape**` attribute to avoid unexpected results.
- Understand Row-major Order: NumPy stores elements in a row-major (C-style) order by default during reshaping. Be mindful of this when working with multi-dimensional arrays.

What to remember:

- -1 for Auto-calculation: You can use `**-1**` in one dimension during reshaping, and NumPy will automatically calculate the size to maintain the original number of elements.

Reshaping is a powerful technique that enhances the flexibility of NumPy arrays, allowing you to adapt your data to different requirements effortlessly.

155. How to access a specific element in a NumPy array?

In NumPy, arrays are like treasure troves of data, and each element is a precious gem waiting to be discovered. We use indexing to access a specific element – a bit like finding the right spot on a map.

Imagine you have a NumPy array named `**my_array**`:

Program code:

```
import numpy as np

my_array = np.array([1, 2, 3, 4, 5])
```

To access the third element (remember, indexing starts from 0), you simply do:

Program code:

```
element = my_array[2]
print(element)
```

What to pay attention to:

- Indexing Starts at 0: Always remember that in Python, the first element has an index of 0, the second has an index of 1, and so on.
- Negative Indexing: Want to start from the end? Use negative indexing. `**-1**` refers to the

last element, `-2` to the second-to-last, and so forth.

Useful tips:

- Slice: To access a range of elements, you can use slicing. For example, **`my_array[1:4]`** gives you elements from index 1 to 3.
- Multi-dimensional Arrays: For arrays with multiple dimensions, like matrices, use a comma-separated index. For a 2D array, **`my_2d_array[1, 2]`** accesses the element in the second row and third column.

156. How can you find the sum of all elements in a NumPy array?

In Python, NumPy is a powerful library for numerical operations, and summing up elements in an array is a common task. Let's dive into

To find the sum of all elements in a NumPy array, you can use the **`numpy.sum()`** function. Here's a quick example:

Program code:

```
import numpy as np

# Creating a NumPy array
my_array = np.array([1, 2, 3, 4, 5])

# Finding the sum of all elements
array_sum = np.sum(my_array)

# Displaying the result
print("Sum of array elements:", array_sum)
```

What to pay attention to:

- The **`numpy.sum()`** function takes the array as its argument and returns the sum of all elements.

Useful tips:

- For multi-dimensional arrays, you can specify the axis along which the sum is calculated. Experiment with the **`axis`** parameter to suit your needs.
- If you're working with a large dataset, consider using the **`np.sum()`** method for faster computation compared to a standard Python loop.

157. What is broadcasting in NumPy?

In NumPy, broadcasting is a powerful feature that enables operations on arrays of different shapes and sizes without explicit looping. This simplifies code and makes it more concise.

Imagine you have two arrays, A and B, with different shapes. Broadcasting allows you to perform element-wise operations on these arrays seamlessly.

Program code:

```
import numpy as np

A = np.array([1, 2, 3])
B = np.array([4, 5, 6])

# Broadcasting in action
result = A + B

print(result)  # Output: [5, 7, 9]
```

Here, NumPy automatically broadcasts the addition operation, making the code clean and efficient.

Key Functions of Broadcasting in NumPy:

1. Implicit Element-Wise Operations:
- Broadcasting allows implicit element-wise operations on arrays with different shapes. It automatically extends the smaller array to match the shape of the larger one.

2. Dimension Compatibility:
- Broadcasting works when dimensions are compatible. It starts from the trailing dimensions and works backward. Dimensions are considered compatible if they are equal or one of them is 1.

3. Unary and Binary Operations:
- Broadcasting applies not only to binary operations (e.g., addition, subtraction) but also to unary operations (e.g., exponentiation, square root). This versatility makes it a powerful tool for various mathematical computations.

4. Efficient Memory Usage:
- Broadcasting promotes efficient memory usage by eliminating the need for explicit loops.

It allows you to perform operations on arrays without creating additional copies, leading to more concise and readable code.

5. Seamless Integration with Scalars:
- Broadcasting seamlessly integrates with scalar values. This means you can perform operations between an array and a scalar without the need to create an array of the same shape as the scalar.

6. Simplified Code:
- One of the primary benefits of broadcasting is code simplification. It reduces the need for manual handling of array shapes, making the code more readable and expressive.

7. Compatible with Universal Functions (ufuncs):
- Broadcasting is compatible with NumPy's universal functions (ufuncs), enabling element-wise operations on arrays while maintaining the efficiency of compiled C code.

8. Trailing Dimension Broadcasting:
- Broadcasting starts from the trailing dimensions and works backward. This approach ensures that operations are consistent across arrays with different shapes and dimensions.

9. Extended Broadcasting Rules:
- Broadcasting rules extend beyond binary operations, covering a wide range of scenarios. Understanding these rules is crucial for effectively utilizing broadcasting in various situations.

10. Versatility Across NumPy Functions:
- Broadcasting is a feature integrated into many NumPy functions, such as arithmetic operations, mathematical functions, and statistical operations. This ensures a consistent and seamless experience when working with different aspects of numerical computing.

158. How do you perform element-wise multiplication of two NumPy arrays?

To multiply elements in two NumPy arrays, you can use the `*` operator. This operation is known as element-wise multiplication, and it's a handy feature for array manipulation in Python.

Program code:

```
import numpy as np

# Create two NumPy arrays
array1 = np.array([1, 2, 3])
array2 = np.array([4, 5, 6])

# Perform element-wise multiplication
result = array1 * array2

print(result)
```

In this example, the result will be `**[4, 10, 18]**`, as each element of `**array1**` is multiplied with the corresponding element of `**array2**`.

What to pay attention to:

- Ensure that the arrays have the same shape. Element-wise operations require arrays to have matching dimensions.
- NumPy automatically performs element-wise operations when using the `**\***` operator, making it a simple and intuitive process.

Useful tips:

- NumPy simplifies array operations, making mathematical operations on arrays concise and efficient.
- Familiarize yourself with other NumPy operations for comprehensive array manipulation.

What to remember:

- Element-wise multiplication is different from matrix multiplication. It operates on corresponding elements of the arrays rather than following matrix multiplication rules.

159. How can you concatenate two NumPy arrays?

When combining two NumPy arrays in Python, use the `**numpy.concatenate()**` function. This function joins arrays along a specified axis, providing flexibility for both 1D and 2D arrays.

Syntax:

```
import numpy as np

result = np.concatenate((array1, array2), axis=0)
```

- **array1** and **array2** are the arrays you want to concatenate.
- **axis=0** specifies concatenation along the rows (vertically). For horizontal concatenation, use **axis=1**.

Program code:

```
import numpy as np

# Creating two arrays
array1 = np.array([1, 2, 3])
array2 = np.array([4, 5, 6])

# Concatenating vertically
result_vertical = np.concatenate((array1, array2), axis=0)

# Concatenating horizontally
result_horizontal = np.concatenate((array1, array2), axis=1)
```

What to pay attention to:

- Ensure that the arrays have compatible shapes along the chosen axis.
- Be cautious with dimensions: 1D arrays concatenate differently than 2D arrays.

Useful tips:

- Explore `**numpy.vstack()**` and `**numpy.hstack()**` for vertical and horizontal stacking, respectively.
- Keep an eye on data types; the arrays should have consistent data types for successful concatenation.

What to remember:

- `**numpy.concatenate()**` is a powerful tool for array combination.
- Choose the axis wisely based on your concatenation needs.

160. How can you transpose a NumPy array?

Transposing a NumPy array is a common operation that swaps its rows and columns. This can be useful in various data manipulation tasks. Let's dive into a simple explanation and provide practical examples.

Syntax:

```
import numpy as np

# Transpose array
transposed_array = np.transpose(original_array)
```

Program code:

```
import numpy as np

original_array = np.array([[1, 2, 3],
                           [4, 5, 6]])
transposed_array = np.transpose(original_array) # Applying the transpose
operation
print(transposed_array)
```

Output:

```
[[1 4]
 [2 5]
 [3 6]]
```

What to pay attention to:

- Transposing doesn't modify the original array; it returns a new transposed array.
- For 1-D arrays, the transpose is equivalent to the original array.

Useful tip:

- When dealing with matrices, transposing can be crucial for certain mathematical operations.

What to remember:

- Use `**np.transpose()**` or the `**.T**` attribute of the array to transpose.
- Transposing multi-dimensional arrays affects the shape.

161. What is the difference between a scalar, vector, and matrix in NumPy?

Scalar:

A scalar in NumPy is a single numerical value, essentially a number. It's the most basic data type and is often used for individual elements in an array.

Program code:

```
scalar_value = 5
print(scalar_value)
```

Remember, a scalar can be created using Python's basic numerical types, like integers or floating-point numbers.

When working with large datasets, scalars are handy for representing individual data points.

Vector:

A vector in NumPy is a one-dimensional array that contains a sequence of scalar values. Think of it as a list of numbers.

Program code:

```
import numpy as np

vector_array = np.array([1, 2, 3, 4, 5])
print(vector_array)
```

Vectors are versatile and commonly used in machine learning for tasks like representing features or labels.

Pay attention to the shape of your vectors. In NumPy, you can check it using the `**shape**` attribute.

Matrix:

A matrix in NumPy is a two-dimensional array that contains a collection of scalar values organized in rows and columns.

Program code:

```
import numpy as np

matrix_array = np.array([[1, 2, 3], [4, 5, 6], [7, 8, 9]])
print(matrix_array)
```

Matrices are powerful for operations involving two dimensions, such as linear transformations.

Use the `**np.dot()**` function for matrix multiplication in NumPy. It's a handy tool when working with matrices.

162. How can you find the maximum value in a NumPy array along a specific axis?

Program code:

```
import numpy as np

# Creating a NumPy array
array_2d = np.array([[1, 2, 3], [4, 5, 6], [7, 8, 9]])

# Finding the maximum along the specified axis (axis=0 in this example)
max_values = np.amax(array_2d, axis=0)

print(max_values)
```

Output:

```
[7 8 9]
```

Specify Axis:

- The `**axis**` parameter determines the axis along which the maximum is calculated. Use `**axis=None**` to find the global maximum.

Useful tip:

- For 1D arrays, specifying the axis is unnecessary as there's only one dimension.
- If unsure about the array shape, use `**array.shape**` to inspect it.
- Be cautious with large datasets; unnecessary calculations can slow down performance.

What to remember:

- Ensure your array is a NumPy array. If not, convert it using `**np.array()**`.

163. Find out the mean, median, and standard deviation of NumPy array

numpy array -> np.array([10, 20, 30, 40, 50, 60])

First, we need to import numpy, a powerful library for numerical computations, using the '**np**' alias:

```
import numpy as np
```

Next, we'll define the numpy array:

```
n1 = np.array([10, 20, 30, 40, 50, 60])
```

Now, let's find the mean, which is the average value of the array:

```
mean_value = np.mean(n1)
print("The mean of the numpy array is:", mean_value)
```

Next up, we'll calculate the median, which represents the middle value of the sorted array:

```
median_value = np.median(n1)
print("The median of the numpy array is:", median_value)
```

Lastly, let's compute the standard deviation, which measures the spread or dispersion of the data:

```
std_deviation = np.std(n1)
print("The standard deviation of the numpy array is:", std_deviation)
```

164. How can you optimize memory usage in a NumPy array?

Memory optimization is crucial when working with NumPy arrays, especially for smooth performance. Let's dive into some practical tips to make the most of your memory:

1. Use Data Types Wisely:

- Choose the right data type for your array elements. Smaller data types (e.g., `**np.int16**` instead of `**np.int32**`) can significantly reduce memory consumption.

Program code:

```
import numpy as np

# Example: Using int16 instead of int32
arr = np.array([1, 2, 3], dtype=np.int16)
```

2. Memory Views with `np.ndarray.view()`:

- Create memory-efficient views of existing arrays using `**view()**`. This can be handy when you need to work with subsets of your data.

Program code:

```
import numpy as np

# Example: Creating a memory view
original_arr = np.array([1, 2, 3, 4, 5])
view_arr = original_arr.view()
```

3. Monitor Memory Usage:

- Keep an eye on your memory usage using tools like `**sys.getsizeof()**` or `**pympler.asizeof()**`. This helps you understand the impact of your optimizations.

Program code:

```
import sys

# Example: Checking memory usage
mem_size = sys.getsizeof(arr)
```

4. Garbage Collection:

- Explicitly release memory using Python's garbage collection (`**gc**` module) if needed, especially when dealing with large arrays in a loop.

Program code:

```
import gc

# Example: Manual garbage collection
gc.collect()
```

What to remember:

- Choosing the right data type is like picking the right-sized box for your belongings - it saves space!
- Views let you peek into your data without the memory commitment of a new array.

165. What is the difference between a shallow copy and a deep copy in NumPy?

Shallow Copy:

In NumPy, a shallow copy creates a new array that references the same data as the original array. Think of it like a pointer to the original data. To make a shallow copy, you can use the `**view()**` method or the slicing operator `**[:]**`. Here's a practical example:

Program code:

```
import numpy as np

original_array = np.array([1, 2, 3])

shallow_copy_1 = original_array.view()
shallow_copy_2 = original_array[:]

# Now, shallow_copy_1 and shallow_copy_2 point to the same data as
original_array.
```

- Shallow copies are memory-efficient but share data with the original array.
- Changes in the original array affect shallow copies, and vice versa.

Deep Copy:

On the other hand, a deep copy creates a completely independent array with its own data. To achieve this, use the `**copy()**` method. Here's an example:

Program code:

```
import numpy as np

original_array = np.array([1, 2, 3])

deep_copy = original_array.copy()

# Now, deep_copy is an entirely new array with its own data, not sharing
anything with original_array.
```

- Deep copies provide data independence, but they might be less memory-efficient.
- Ideal when you need a separate copy with no connection to the original array.

Understanding when to use shallow or deep copies depends on your specific needs. If memory efficiency is critical and changes in one should reflect in others, go for a shallow copy. A deep copy is the way to go if you need complete independence.

166. Explain the data types supported by NumPy

Explore the diverse data types supported by NumPy to enhance your Python skills. Familiarize yourself with the following types and their corresponding aliases:

- `**numpy.bool_**`: Boolean data type.
- `**numpy.byte**`: Signed char data type.
- `**numpy.ubyte**`: Unsigned char data type.
- `**numpy.short**`: Short integer data type.
- `**numpy.ushort**`: Unsigned short integer data type.
- `**numpy.intc**`: Integer data type.
- `**numpy.uintc**`: Unsigned integer data type.
- `**numpy.int_**`: Long integer data type.
- `**numpy.uint**`: Unsigned long integer data type.
- `**numpy.longlong**`: Long long integer data type.
- `**numpy.ulonglong**`: Unsigned long long integer data type.
- `**numpy.half**` / `**numpy.float16**`: Half precision float data type.
- `**numpy.single**`: Single precision float data type.
- `**numpy.double**`: Double precision float data type.
- `**numpy.longdouble**`: Long double precision float data type.
- `**numpy.csingle**`: Complex single precision float data type.
- `**numpy.cdouble**`: Complex double precision float data type.
- `**numpy.clongdouble**`: Complex long double precision float data type.

Program code:

```
import numpy as np

# Boolean
bool_var = np.array(True, dtype=np.bool_)

# Signed char
byte_var = np.array(65, dtype=np.byte)

# Unsigned char
ubyte_var = np.array(120, dtype=np.ubyte)
```

```
# Short
short_var = np.array(-32768, dtype=np.short)

# Unsigned short
ushort_var = np.array(65535, dtype=np.ushort)

# Int
int_var = np.array(-2147483648, dtype=np.intc)

# Unsigned int
uint_var = np.array(4294967295, dtype=np.uintc)

# Long
long_var = np.array(-9223372036854775808, dtype=np.int_)

# Unsigned long
ulong_var = np.array(18446744073709551615, dtype=np.uint)

# Long long
longlong_var = np.array(-9223372036854775808, dtype=np.longlong)

# Unsigned long long
ulonglong_var = np.array(18446744073709551615, dtype=np.ulonglong)

# Half precision float
half_var = np.array(3.14, dtype=np.half)

# Single precision float
single_var = np.array(3.14, dtype=np.single)

# Double precision float
double_var = np.array(3.14, dtype=np.double)

# Long double precision float
longdouble_var = np.array(3.14, dtype=np.longdouble)

# Complex single precision float
csingle_var = np.array(3.14 + 2j, dtype=np.csingle)

# Complex double precision float
cdouble_var = np.array(3.14 + 2j, dtype=np.cdouble)
```

```
# Complex long double precision float
clongdouble_var = np.array(3.14 + 2j, dtype=np.clongdouble)
```

What to pay attention to:

- Be mindful of the specific data type required for your application to optimize memory usage and performance.
- Python automatically infers data types, but explicit specification can prevent unexpected behavior.

What to remember:

- NumPy provides a wide range of data types to suit various numerical computations.
- Choose the appropriate data type based on the range and precision of your data.

Useful tips:

- Explore the NumPy documentation for additional details on each data type and their applications.
- Experiment with different data types to understand their impact on computational efficiency.

167. Why is the shape property used in NumPy?

In NumPy, the `**shape**` property is your go-to tool for uncovering the dimensions of an array. It's like a blueprint that tells you how many elements are packed into each dimension.

Program code:

```
import numpy as np

example = np.array([[1, 2, 3, 4], [5, 6, 7, 8]])
print(example.shape)
```

When you run this, you'll get an output like `**(2, 4)**`. Now, don't let those parentheses intimidate you – they're just signaling that we're dealing with 2 dimensions here, and each dimension is rocking 4 elements.

What to pay attention to:

- The `**shape**` property is your guide to the array's structure.
- The first number represents the number of rows (dimensions), and the second is the number of elements in each row.

What to remember:

- The order matters. In our example, `**(2, 4)**` means 2 rows and 4 elements in each row.

168. How can you create a diagonal matrix in NumPy?

Creating a diagonal matrix in NumPy is straightforward, thanks to the handy diag function. This type of matrix is square, with all non-diagonal elements set to zero. Whether you're working with a 1D array or a scalar, NumPy's got you covered.

Program code:

```
import numpy as np

# Creating a diagonal matrix with elements [1, 2, 3] on the diagonal
diagonal_matrix = np.diag([1, 2, 3])
```

- **Array or Scalar:** Whether you provide an array or a single value, np.diag() adapts and crafts a diagonal matrix for you.

- **Square Shape:** Diagonal matrices are square, so the number of elements you provide determines the size of your matrix.

169. How do you calculate the covariance matrix in NumPy?

Calculating the covariance matrix in NumPy is a breeze using the cov() function. This handy function allows you to swiftly compute the covariance matrix for a set of variables. Let's dive into a quick example:

Program code:

```
import numpy as np

# Assume x and y are your variables
data = np.array([x, y])

covariance_matrix = np.cov(data)
```

The cov() function takes care of the heavy lifting, giving you a matrix that showcases the covariances between different pairs of variables.

Ensure your data is organized in a NumPy array for seamless computation.

Pay attention to the fact that the resulting matrix is symmetric. The element in the ith row and jth column is the covariance between the ith and jth variables.

NumPy's cov() function streamlines the process, allowing you to focus on understanding the relationships within your data.

170. Understanding `vstack()` in NumPy

`**vstack()**` is a function in NumPy, short for `**vertical stack**`. As the name suggests, it's used to stack arrays vertically, i.e., along the rows.

Imagine you have two arrays:

Program code:

```
array1 = np.array([1, 2, 3])
array2 = np.array([4, 5, 6])
```

By using `**vstack()**`, you can combine these two arrays into a single one vertically:

Program code:

```
combined_array = np.vstack((array1, array2))
print(combined_array)
```

Output:

```
[[1 2 3]
[4 5 6]]
```

Useful tips and What to remember:

- The arrays you want to stack must have the same shape along all but the first axis.
- `**vstack()**` can be especially handy when you're aggregating data from multiple sources with the same columns or features.
- If you need to stack arrays horizontally, you can use `**hstack()**`.

171. What is the difference between NumPy and SciPy in Python?

NumPy, short for Numerical Python, and SciPy, short for Scientific Python, are two essential tools in Python. They may sound similar, but they serve different purposes.

NumPy is like the foundation of a house. It's the go-to library for dealing with arrays and tackling straightforward mathematical tasks. Imagine you have a list of numbers and want to perform operations on them – that's where NumPy shines.

SciPy, on the other hand, is like the toolbox you use to build complex machines. It's designed to tackle more intricate challenges like numerical integration, optimization, and machine learning. When your Python code needs to solve scientific and engineering problems that go beyond basic math, SciPy steps in.

Suppose you want to calculate the mean and standard deviation of a list of exam scores in Python. You'd turn to **NumPy** for this task because it excels at handling arrays and basic statistics:

Program code:

```
import numpy as np

scores = [85, 92, 78, 90, 88]
mean_score = np.mean(scores)
std_deviation = np.std(scores)

print("Mean Score:", mean_score)
print("Standard Deviation:", std_deviation)
```

But if you're working on something more advanced, like simulating a physical system or optimizing a complex mathematical function, you'd dive into **SciPy**:

Program code:

```
import scipy.integrate as spi

# Define the function to integrate
def my_function(x):
    return x**2

result, _ = spi.quad(my_function, 0, 1)

print("Integral Result:", result)
```

So, in a nutshell, NumPy handles the basics, while SciPy is your companion for scientific and engineering challenges. Both are incredibly valuable in Python, depending on what kind of problem you're solving.

Python Frameworks

172. What are Frameworks in Python?

In Python, frameworks are powerful tools that simplify and expedite the development of applications. They provide a structured foundation, allowing you to focus on your application's logic rather than dealing with low-level details. Let's explore this concept with clarity and practical insights.

Frameworks in Python are pre-built structures that offer a set of conventions, guidelines, and reusable code to streamline application development. They provide a scaffold, enabling developers to build robust and scalable software efficiently.

Consider Flask and Django, two popular Python frameworks. Flask is a micro-framework, perfect for small to medium-sized projects, while Django, a full-stack framework, is suitable for larger applications. Flask's simplicity is evident in its minimalistic design, making it easy for beginners to grasp. On the other hand, Django offers many built-in features, reducing the need for manual configurations.

What to pay attention to:

- When choosing a framework, consider the project requirements. Flask is ideal for lightweight applications, while Django suits complex projects with more built-in functionalities. Understanding your project's scope helps in making an informed decision.

Useful tips:

- Start with a micro-framework like Flask for more straightforward projects.
- Explore the documentation to understand the framework's features and best practices.
- Join the community – forums and discussion groups are excellent resources for learning and problem-solving.

What to remember:

- Frameworks handle everyday tasks like URL routing, database interactions, and form handling, allowing you to focus on unique aspects of your application. Familiarize yourself with a framework's documentation to leverage its capabilities effectively.

Python frameworks empower developers by providing a structured foundation for building applications.

173. What is Django, and how is it used for web development?

Django is a powerful framework that simplifies web development in Python. It streamlines the creation of robust, scalable, and maintainable web applications. Let's break down the key aspects:

1. Django fundamentals:

Django follows the Model-View-Controller (MVC) architectural pattern, which is essential to comprehend.

What to pay attention to:

- Understand the role of models (data representation), views (user interface), and controllers (application logic) in your web application.

2. Creating a Django project:

To start, you'll need to set up a Django project. Here's a quick example:

Program code:

```
django-admin startproject myproject
```

What to remember:

- The project serves as the container for your entire application. Pay attention to the project structure and files it generates.

3. Building Django apps:

Django organizes functionality into apps. For instance, if you're creating a blog within your project:

Program code:

```
python manage.py startapp blog
```

Useful tip:

- Apps help modularize your project, making it more scalable and maintainable.

4. Defining models:

Models represent your data. When designing a blog, consider creating a model for posts:

Program code:

```
from django.db import models

class Post(models.Model):
    title = models.CharField(max_length=100)
    content = models.TextField()
```

What to pay attention to:

- Models define the structure of your database. Ensure clarity in data representation.

5. Creating views and templates:

Views handle user requests and return appropriate responses. Templates define how data is presented. For a blog post:

Program code:

```
# views.py
from django.shortcuts import render
from .models import Post

def post_list(request):
    posts = Post.objects.all()
    return render(request, 'blog/post_list.html', {'posts': posts})
```

Useful tip:

- Keep views lightweight by delegating complex logic to models.

6. URL patterns:

Mapping URLs to views is crucial. Specify patterns in your app's `**urls.py**`:

Program code:

```
# urls.py
from django.urls import path
from .views import post_list

urlpatterns = [
    path('posts/', post_list, name='post_list'),
]
```

What to remember:

- Clear URL patterns enhance the user experience.

7. Running the development server:
To test your application, run the development server:

Program code:
```
python manage.py runserver
```

Useful tip:
- Regularly check the console for any error messages or warnings.

Django empowers you to build dynamic web applications efficiently. Focus on mastering the MVC pattern, creating modular apps, and understanding the role of models, views, and templates.

174. Discuss the importance of Flask in web application development

Flask, a lightweight and powerful framework, plays a pivotal role in web application development with Python. Let's dive into its significance, highlighting practical examples, key points to focus on, and tips to keep in mind, all tailored for beginners.

Understanding Flask's significance:

Flask empowers developers to create web applications efficiently. Its simplicity and flexibility make it a favorite among beginners and seasoned developers. Here's a breakdown to help you grasp its importance:

Program code:
```
# Example 1: Hello World in Flask
from flask import Flask
app = Flask(__name__)

@app.route('/')
def hello_world():
    return 'Hello, World!'

if __name__ == '__main__':
    app.run()
```

This essential "Hello World" example demonstrates the core structure of a Flask application.

The `**@app.route('/')**` decorator defines a route, and the associated function handles the logic for that route.

What to pay attention to:

- Routes and Views: Understand how routes map to different views in your application. Routes are crucial for directing users to specific functionalities.
- Templates: Flask integrates seamlessly with templates (HTML files), allowing you to separate your application's logic and presentation.
- Extensions: Explore Flask extensions to enhance functionality. Popular extensions include Flask-SQLAlchemy for database interactions and Flask-WTF for form handling.

Useful tips:

- Documentation is Your Friend: Flask has excellent documentation. Refer to it regularly for in-depth explanations and examples.
- Leverage Flask Blueprints: As your application grows, use Flask Blueprints to organize your code into manageable components.

What to remember:

- Keep It Modular: Break down your application into modular components. This enhances maintainability and makes it easier to scale your project.
- Use Virtual Environments: Create isolated environments for your projects using `**virtualenv**` to avoid conflicts between dependencies.

Embrace the simplicity of Flask as you embark on your web development journey. Don't hesitate to explore its vast community and resources to enrich your learning experience.

In summary, Flask is a game-changer in web development, offering a clean and efficient way to build robust applications. By focusing on practical examples and key principles, you'll master Flask and create impressive web solutions quickly.

175. Explain what Flask is and its benefits?

Flask is a fantastic open-source web framework that provides all the tools and technologies you need to build amazing online applications. Whether creating a simple web page, a wiki, a feature-rich web-based calendar software, or a full-fledged commercial website, Flask has got you covered!

One of the best things about Flask is that it's a micro-framework, which means it doesn't burden you with unnecessary dependencies on other libraries. This makes Flask lightweight and efficient, perfect for easily developing web applications.

Now, let's talk about the benefits of using Flask:

Built-in unit testing support

Flask comes with integrated unit testing support, making it easier for developers to ensure the reliability and stability of their applications.

Convenient development server and debugger

Flask provides a built-in development server and a rapid debugger, making the development process smoother and less error-prone.

Restful request dispatch

You can efficiently handle Restful requests with Flask, and it's based on Unicode, making it accessible to a diverse audience.

Easy cookie handling

Working with cookies is a breeze in Flask, giving you more flexibility in managing user sessions and preferences.

Jinja2 templating

Flask is compatible with WSGI 1.0 and uses the powerful jinja2 templating engine, making it a joy to create dynamic and appealing web pages.

Complete project control

With Flask, you have complete control over your project's progress. Customize it the way you want and bring your ideas to life effortlessly.

HTTP request processing

Flask simplifies HTTP request processing, allowing you to focus on the core functionality of your application.

Lightweight and versatile

As a lightweight framework, Flask is easy to integrate with various extensions, making it adaptable to different project requirements.

Device-friendly

Flask makes connecting with your favorite devices easy, ensuring a seamless experience for your users, no matter their platform.

Well-designed API

The API for ORM Basic is thoughtfully designed and organized, making database interactions smooth and efficient.

Highly flexible

Flask is incredibly flexible, enabling you to tailor your web application precisely as you envision it.

In conclusion, Flask is an amazing web framework that combines simplicity, power, and flexibility.

176. Is Django better than Flask?

Well, both are excellent Python web frameworks, each with its own strengths!

Let's talk about Django first. It's incredibly popular because it comes with a ton of built-in functionality, which makes it perfect for handling complex applications. If you're working on a larger project with lots of features, Django might be the right choice for you. However, for smaller applications, some of these features might feel like overkill.

Now, let's dive into Flask. If you're new to web programming, Flask is an amazing starting point. Many developers love using Flask, and it powers quite a number of websites, though not as many as Django. Flask offers you more precise control over your web application, making it a favorite for developers who want to fine-tune every aspect of their project.

Ultimately, the choice between Django and Flask depends on your project's specific needs. If you're looking for a well-rounded and feature-rich framework, Django might be your best bet. On the other hand, if you prefer a lightweight and flexible framework that allows you to have more control, Flask could be the perfect fit.

177. Mention the differences between Django, Pyramid, and Flask

When it comes to Python web frameworks like Django, Pyramid, and Flask, it's essential to understand their unique characteristics. Let's take a closer look at the key differences between these frameworks:

Django:

- Django is a powerful Python web framework designed for building large-scale applications.
- It comes with an Object-Relational Mapping (ORM) system by default, making it easy to interact with databases.
- Django follows the "batteries-included" philosophy, providing a wide range of built-in

components and tools out of the box.

- It is an excellent choice for developers who prefer an all-in-one solution for their web projects.

Pyramid:

- Pyramid is a flexible and versatile Python web framework, that focuses on giving developers the freedom to choose the best tools for their specific project needs.
- Unlike Django, it does not impose a specific ORM or database approach, allowing developers to work with the persistence layer of their choice.
- Pyramid is adaptable and works well with various databases, including popular options like SQLAlchemy, as well as emerging ones like DynamoDB and MongoDB.

Flask:

- Flask, on the other hand, is a lightweight "micro-framework" designed for smaller applications with fewer requirements.
- It offers developers the core essentials to get started without any unnecessary features or components.
- Flask does not come with an ORM or other built-in tools, allowing developers to choose the specific libraries they need for their projects.

To summarize:

- Django is ideal for large-scale projects with its extensive feature set and included ORM.
- Pyramid prioritizes flexibility, allowing developers to customize their project stack as needed.
- Flask is perfect for smaller applications where simplicity and minimalism are key.

When choosing a web framework for your Python project, consider your specific requirements, the size of the application, and your preferred level of flexibility. Each of these frameworks has its strengths, making them valuable tools for different types of web development projects.

178. Discuss Django architecture

Django follows a popular design pattern called MVC, which stands for Model-View-Controller. This architectural approach divides the framework into three essential parts:

Model:

In Django, the Model represents the logical data structure of your application. Think of it as the backbone that supports the entire program. Typically, Django uses relational databases like MySQL or PostgreSQL to store this data. So, when you interact with your application, it's the

Model that manages the data behind the scenes.

View:
The View is what you see when you visit a website powered by Django. It's the user interface—the part that you interact with in your browser. To create the Views, Django uses HTML, CSS, and JavaScript files. These files define how the data from the Model should be presented to users, making the whole experience visually appealing and user-friendly.

Controller:
The Controller acts as the bridge between the Model and the View. Its primary responsibility is to transfer data from the Model to the View and vice versa. When you request something from your application, the Controller handles the logic, retrieves the necessary data from the Model, and sends it to the appropriate View for display.

So, in a nutshell, when you work with Django using the MVC architecture, your application revolves around the Model. It's the underlying data structure that you'll be either displaying to users or modifying as needed. The Controller manages the flow of information, while the View ensures that everything looks great and works smoothly for the end-users.

Understanding Django's MVC architecture is crucial for any Python developer, especially when preparing for interviews. It showcases Django's elegance and power in organizing code and simplifying the development process."

179. Setting up a database in Django

Django makes it easy to set up a database for your project. In the `**settings.py**` file, you'll find all the essential configurations for your database connection. By default, Django uses SQLite, but it can be configured to work with other databases too.

Let's walk through setting up a MySQL database in Django. First, make sure you have the `**django.db.backends.mysql**` driver installed.

In your `**settings.py**` file, you'll add the database configuration like this:

Program code:

```
DATABASES = {
    'default': {
        'ENGINE': 'django.db.backends.mysql',
        'NAME': 'djangoApp',
        'USER': 'root',
        'PASSWORD': 'mysql',
        'HOST': 'localhost',
        'PORT': '3306'
    }
}
```

Useful tips:

- The `**ENGINE**` specifies the database backend to use.
- `**NAME**` is the database name.
- `**USER**` and `**PASSWORD**` are your database login credentials.
- `**HOST**` is where your database is hosted.
- `**PORT**` is the port your database server listens on.

What to remember:

- Database setup in Django requires specific connection details, including the database name, user credentials, hostname, and driver name.

With this configuration, you can now create tables for `**admin**`, `**auth**`, `**content_types**`, and `**sessions**` in your MySQL database. You can select it from the database drop-down menu and start building your application with a solid database foundation.

Setting up a database in Django is a fundamental step, and with this example, you're on your way to building robust web applications!

180. How to create a Django view?

In Django, views are an essential part of the Model-View-Template (MVT) structure. Think of a view as a Python function that handles web requests and generates web responses. These responses can be web page content, redirects, error messages, XML data, images, and more. They essentially decide what your users see in their web browsers.

Creating a Simple View.

Here's an example of a basic Django view:

Program code:

```
# Import HttpResponse from Django
from django.http import HttpResponse

# Import datetime
import datetime

# Define a function for your view
def my_view(request):
    # Get the current date and time
    now = datetime.datetime.now()

    # Create an HTML message with the current time
    html = "The current time is: {}".format(now)

    # Return the HTML message as a response
    return HttpResponse(html)
```

Code explanation:

- We import `**HttpResponse**` from Django to help generate a response.
- We import `**datetime**` to work with date and time.
- We define a function (`**my_view**`) that takes a `**request**` as an argument.
- Inside the function, we obtain the current date and time.
- We create an HTML message containing the time.
- Finally, we return this HTML message as a response.

What to remember:

- Views are crucial in how your web application interacts with users. They handle user requests and prepare the content users see in their web browsers. This is just a basic example to get you started. You can create more complex views to build the functionality you need for your Django project.

181. How sessions work in Django

In Django, sessions are a handy way to keep track of user data and preferences across web requests. They allow you to save and retrieve information per user, making it available every time they interact with your website. Think of sessions as a personal notepad for each user, storing their data securely.

Enabling sessions

In a Django project, sessions are enabled by default. You don't need to worry about complicated configurations. You can find session settings in your project's `**settings.py**` file under the `**INSTALLED_APPS**` and `**MIDDLEWARE**` sections.

Program code:

```
# settings.py
INSTALLED_APPS = [
    ...
    'django.contrib.sessions',
    ...
]

MIDDLEWARE = [
    ...
    'django.contrib.sessions.middleware.SessionMiddleware',
    ...
]
```

By default, Django stores session data in the database, which is a secure and reliable option.

Using sessions

To work with sessions, you can access the `**request**` object in your views. This object contains a `**session**` property, which allows you to interact with the session data. The session data is associated with the user's browser, and Django handles the connection details for you.

You can perform various operations on the session data using a dictionary-like approach:

1. Getting session data

Program code:

```
# Get a session value using its key, raising a KeyError if the key is not
present
my_bike = request.session['my_bike']

# Get a session value, setting a default value if it's not present
my_bike = request.session.get('my_bike', 'mini')
```

2. Setting session data

Program code:
```
# Set a session value
request.session['my_bike'] = 'mini'
```

3. Deleting session data

Program code:
```
# Delete a session value
del request.session['my_bike']
```

Django offers a variety of methods in its API to manage session cookies. You can check if the user's browser supports cookies, set and check cookie expiration dates, and even delete expired sessions from the data store. For more details, consult the Django documentation on sessions.

The beauty of Django is that it takes care of the session-handling mechanisms behind the scenes, allowing you to focus on building your web application.

182. List out the inheritance styles in Django

In Django, there are several inheritance styles you can use. Let's break them down into practical examples and key points to remember.

Abstract base classes

In Django, you can use abstract base classes when you want a parent class to hold common data that you don't want to redefine for each child model. Here's an example:

Program code:
```
from django.db import models

class ContactInfo(models.Model):
    name = models.CharField(max_length=20)
    email = models.EmailField(max_length=20)
    address = models.TextField(max_length=20)

    class Meta:
        abstract = True
```

```
class Customer(ContactInfo):
    phone = models.IntegerField(max_length=15)

class Staff(ContactInfo):
    position = models.CharField(max_length=10)
```

What to remember:

- Abstract base classes are used to store common fields.
- Child models inherit fields and add their own.

Multi-table inheritance

Multi-table inheritance is used when you want each subclass to have its own database table. Here's an example:

Program code:

```
from django.db import models

class Place(models.Model):
    name = models.CharField(max_length=20)
    address = models.TextField(max_length=20)

    def __str__(self):
        return self.name

class Restaurant(Place):
    serves_pizza = models.BooleanField(default=False)
    serves_pasta = models.BooleanField(default=False)

    def __str__(self):
        return self.name
```

What to remember:

- Each subclass gets its own database table.
- Fields are inherited from the parent class.

Proxy models

Proxy models are used to change the behavior of a model at the Python level without altering the model's fields. You can add new methods and properties. However, you cannot change the model's fields themselves.

What to remember:

- Use proxy models to customize a model's behavior without altering fields.
- You inherit from the base class and add your own methods.
- You cannot use abstract classes as base classes.
- Multiple inheritance is not allowed in proxy models.

Program code:

```
from django.db import models

class Place(models.Model):
    name = models.CharField(max_length=20)
    address = models.TextField(max_length=20)

    def __str__(self):
        return self.name

class PlaceProxy(Place):
    class Meta:
        proxy = True

    def custom_method(self):
        return f"Custom method for {self.name}"
```

Use these inheritance styles wisely in your Django projects to create efficient and structured models.

Advanced Topics

183. What are Python decorators?

Python decorators are a powerful tool that allow you to modify or enhance the behavior of functions or methods in a clean and organized way. Think of them as wrappers for your functions, giving them extra capabilities without changing their core code. Here's What to remember:

What are decorators?

Decorators are functions themselves, and they're typically used to modify other functions. You apply decorators to functions using the `**@** ` symbol above the function definition.

Let's say you have a function that calculates the square of a number:

Program code:

```
def square(x):
    return x * x
```

You can create a decorator to log when the function is called:

Program code:

```
def log_function_call(func):
    def wrapper(*args, **kwargs):
        result = func(*args, **kwargs)
        print(f"Function {func.__name__} was called with arguments {args}
and returned {result}")
        return result
    return wrapper
```

Now, you can use the `**@log_function_call**` decorator to log every call to the `**square**` function like this:

Program code:

```
@log_function_call
def square(x):
    return x * x

square(4)
```

Output:

```
Function square was called with arguments (4,) and returned 16
```

What to pay attention to:

- Decorators should take a function as an argument and return a new function.
- Decorators are an excellent way to separate concerns and keep your code clean.

Useful tip:

- Python has some built-in decorators like `**@staticmethod**`, `**@classmethod**`, and `**@property**` that you'll commonly encounter in object-oriented programming.

Decorators are a fantastic way to add extra functionality to your functions without cluttering their code. They're like the icing on the Python cake, making your code more readable and maintainable. So, don't be afraid to use them!

184. Explain the concept of generators and iterators

In Python, generators and iterators play key roles in enhancing code efficiency and readability. They empower you to work with large datasets or streams of information without loading everything into memory at once. Let's break down these concepts with clarity and practicality.

Understanding iterators:

An iterator is like a magic wand for looping through elements in a collection, such as a list or a tuple. It simplifies moving through each item without indexing or keeping track manually. Take a look at this concise example:

Program code:

```
# Creating an iterator
my_list = [1, 2, 3, 4, 5]
my_iterator = iter(my_list)

# Looping through the iterator
for item in my_iterator:
    print(item)
```

What to remember:

- Use the `**iter()**` function to create an iterator from a collection.
- Employ the `**next()**` function to move through the iterator step by step.

Generator magic:

Now, let's elevate our game with generators. A generator is a special kind of iterator that allows you to create an iterable sequence on-the-fly. Unlike traditional functions that return values, generators use the `**yield**` keyword to produce a series of values, pausing and resuming execution as needed.

Program code:

```
# Creating a simple generator
def count_up_to(limit):
    count = 1
    while count <= limit:
        yield count
        count += 1

# Using the generator
for number in count_up_to(5):
    print(number)
```

Useful tips:

- Consider efficient memory usage when creating iterators or generators, especially when dealing with extensive data.
- The `**yield**` statement is the secret sauce for generators. It allows you to pause the function and resume where it left off.

What to remember:

- Generators are memory-efficient and ideal for handling large datasets or infinite sequences.

185. How does multithreading work in Python?

Multithreading in Python opens up a world of simultaneous execution, enabling your code to juggle multiple tasks seamlessly. Let's dive into the essentials with practical insights, pointers, and beginner-friendly tips.

Understanding multithreading:

In Python, multithreading allows you to execute multiple threads concurrently, boosting performance for tasks like I/O operations. It's important to note that due to the Global Interpreter Lock (GIL), Python threads might not achieve true parallelism for CPU-bound tasks.

Creating threads:

To embark on your multithreading adventure, utilize the `**threading**` module. Here's a quick snippet to create an essential thread:

Program code:

```
import threading

def my_function():
    # Your task goes here

# Create a thread
my_thread = threading.Thread(target=my_function)
```

Starting threads:

Once created, kickstart your threads into action using the `**start()**` method:

Program code:

```
my_thread.start()
```

Useful tips:

- I/O Operations Shine: Multithreading excels in scenarios with I/O-bound operations, like network requests or file handling.
- Thread Lifecycle: Understand the lifecycle of a thread: creation, start, join, and termination.

What to remember:

- GIL Constraints: Python's GIL may limit parallel execution for CPU-bound tasks. Consider multiprocessing for such scenarios.
- Thread Safety: Pay attention to shared resources to prevent data conflicts. Utilize locks (`**threading.Lock()**`) for synchronization.

- Multithreading is a powerful tool, but its optimal use depends on the nature of your tasks. For CPU-bound operations, explore the multiprocessing module for a more parallel-friendly approach.

186. What is a classifier?

Its job is to predict the `**class**` or category of a data point. Imagine you have a bunch of pictures of animals, and you want to know if each picture shows a cat, dog, or bird. That's where classifiers come in!

Think of classifiers as little detectives. They use special techniques and `**training data**` (kind of like study material) to understand the relationship between different features (or input variables) and the classes they belong to. Once they learn enough from this training, they can confidently label new data points.

By the way, classification is a key part of supervised learning in Machine Learning. In this approach, the model is taught using labeled examples, meaning it knows the right answers beforehand. As a result, the classifier can become quite accurate at sorting things into the correct categories!

187. What are the tools present to perform static analysis?

When it comes to examining Python code for potential issues, there are two prominent tools in the realm of static analysis: Pychecker and Pylint.

Pychecker takes on the role of a bug detective within your source code. It actively identifies bugs and irregularities, ensuring the integrity of your codebase. Beyond that, Pychecker extends its functionality to assess the style and complexity of your code, offering insights into how well it aligns with best practices.

On the other hand, **Pylint** serves as a coding standards enforcer. It meticulously examines your Python modules, evaluating them against predefined coding standards. This diligent process ensures that your code maintains a consistent and uniform structure, which is essential for readability, maintainability, and collaboration within a development team.

In summary, these two static analysis tools, **Pychecker** and **Pylint**, play a pivotal role in enhancing the quality and reliability of Python code by detecting bugs, promoting good coding practices, and ensuring adherence to established coding standards.

188. How can you create a bar plot?

How can you create a bar plot for the top 5 states with the highest number of confirmed COVID-19 cases as of July 17, 2020, using a given dataset?

Making a bar plot for the top 5 states with the highest number of confirmed COVID-19 cases is a common task in data analysis. Here's a step-by-step guide with some practical tips and explanations:

STEP 1: PREPARE THE DATA

- First, we need to select the relevant columns from the dataset. These columns include `**Date**`, `**State/UnionTerritory**`, `**Cured**`, `**Deaths**`, and `**Confirmed**`. We can achieve this with the following code:

Program code:

```
df = df[['Date', 'State/UnionTerritory', 'Cured', 'Deaths', 'Confirmed']]
```

Useful tip:

- It's essential to focus on the necessary data columns to keep your analysis efficient.

STEP 2: RENAME THE COLUMNS

- Renaming the columns makes the data more readable. In this case, we'll rename the columns as follows:

Program code:

```
df.columns = ['date', 'state', 'cured', 'deaths', 'confirmed']
```

Useful tip:

- Clear and meaningful column names improve code readability.

STEP 3: SELECT DATA FOR THE DESIRED DATE

- We want to analyze data as of July 17, 2020. To do this, we'll extract records for that specific date:

Program code:

```
today = df[df.date == '2020-07-17']
```

STEP 4: SORT DATA BY CONFIRMED CASES

- To find the states with the highest number of confirmed cases, we'll sort the data in descending order based on the `**confirmed**` column:

Program code:

```
    max_confirmed_cases = today.sort_values(by='confirmed',
ascending=False)
```

STEP 5: GET THE TOP 5 STATES

- We'll select the top 5 states with the highest number of confirmed cases:

Program code:

```
    top_states_confirmed = max_confirmed_cases[:5]
```

STEP 6: CREATE THE BAR PLOT

- To visualize the top 5 states, we'll use the Seaborn library to create a bar plot. The `**state**` column will be mapped to the x-axis, and the `**confirmed**` column will be mapped to the y-axis. The `**state**` column will also determine the color of the bars.

Program code:

```
    import seaborn as sns
    import matplotlib.pyplot as plt

    sns.set(rc={'figure.figsize': (15, 10)})
    sns.barplot(x='state', y='confirmed', data=top_states_confirmed,
hue='state')
    plt.show()
```

Useful tip:

- Data visualization is a powerful tool for understanding and presenting your findings.

In summary, following these steps, you can create a bar plot that effectively displays the top 5 states with the highest number of confirmed COVID-19 cases as of July 17, 2020, from the given dataset.

189. How to create a bar plot?

How to create a bar plot for the top 5 States with the Most COVID-19 Deaths?

To visualize the COVID-19 dataset and create a bar plot for the top 5 states with the highest number of deaths, follow these steps:

Program code:

```
import seaborn as sns
import matplotlib.pyplot as plt

#Step 1: Sort the data by the "deaths" column in descending order
max_death_cases = today.sort_values(by="deaths", ascending=False)

#Step 2: Set the plot's figure size
sns.set(rc={'figure.figsize': (15, 10)}

#Step 3: Create the bar plot
sns.barplot(x="state", y="deaths", data=max_death_cases.head(5),
hue="state")

#Step 4: Display the plot
plt.show()
```

Code explanation:

- We begin by sorting our dataset based on the `**deaths**` column in descending order, ensuring the states with the highest death counts come first:

Program code:

```
max_death_cases = today.sort_values(by="deaths", ascending=False)
```

- Next, we adjust the figure size for our plot using Seaborn's `**sns.set()**`. This step helps in creating a visually appealing and informative bar plot:

Program code:

```
sns.set(rc={'figure.figsize': (15, 10)})
```

- To create the bar plot, we use Seaborn's `**sns.barplot()**` function. We map the `**state**` column to the x-axis and the `**deaths**` column to the y-axis. The `**hue**` parameter is used to distinguish between the states in the plot:

Program code:

```
sns.barplot(x="state", y="deaths", data=max_death_cases.head(5),
hue="state")
```

- Finally, we display the bar plot with `**plt.show()**`.

This code generates a bar plot that showcases the top 5 states with the highest COVID-19 death counts, helping you visualize the data effectively.

190. How can you create a line plot?

How can you create a line plot to show the confirmed COVID-19 cases over time from a dataset, specifically for the state of Florida?

Program code:

```
import pandas as pd
import seaborn as sns
import matplotlib.pyplot as plt

# Step 1: Filter data for Florida
florida = df[df.state == 'Florida']

# Step 2: Set the plot size
sns.set(rc={'figure.figsize': (15, 10)})

# Step 3: Create the line plot
sns.lineplot(x="date", y="confirmed", data= florida, color="g")

# Step 4: Display the plot
plt.show()
```

Code explanation:

- First, we filter the dataset to include only records related to the state of Florida:

Program code:

```
florida = df[df.state == 'Florida']
```

- We set the size of the plot using seaborn to make it more visually appealing:

Program code:

```
sns.set(rc={'figure.figsize': (15, 10)})
```

- Next, we create the line plot using seaborn, mapping the `**date**` column to the x-axis and the `**confirmed**` column to the y-axis. We use the color `**g**` for the line (green):

Program code:

```
sns.lineplot(x="date", y="confirmed", data=flo, color="g")
```

- Finally, we display the plot with `**plt.show()**`, allowing you to visualize the trend in confirmed COVID-19 cases over time in Florida.

191. How to implement linear regression on the "Florida" dataset?

In this scenario, we want to use a linear regression algorithm to predict the number of confirmed cases based on the `**date**` as the independent variable.

Here's how to do it:

Program code:

```
# Import the necessary libraries
from sklearn.model_selection import train_test_split
from sklearn.linear_model import LinearRegression

# Convert the date to ordinal format
florida['date'] = florida['date'].map(dt.datetime.toordinal)

# Divide the dataset into training and testing sets
x = florida['date']
y = florida['confirmed']
x_train, x_test, y_train, y_test = train_test_split(x, y, test_size=0.3)
```

```
# Build the linear regression model
lr = LinearRegression()
lr.fit(np.array(x_train).reshape(-1, 1), np.array(y_train).reshape(-1, 1))

# Make predictions for a specific date (e.g., 737630)
prediction = lr.predict(np.array([[737630]])
```

Code explanation:

- We start by converting the "date" column to an ordinal format. This step is essential because linear regression models require numerical data, not dates.

- Next, we split our dataset into training and testing sets using the `**train_test_split**` function. This division allows us to train the model on one subset and evaluate its performance on another.

- We create an instance of the LinearRegression model and fit it with the training data. The `**.fit()**` method trains the model to understand the relationship between the date and the number of confirmed cases.

- Finally, we can use the trained model to make predictions. In this example, we predict the number of confirmed cases for a specific date, which is 737630.

Useful tip:

- You can further improve your model by exploring different features or using more advanced regression techniques if needed.

What to remember:

- Linear regression is a simple yet powerful tool for predicting numerical outcomes based on one or more input variables. Ensure your data is properly preprocessed and that you understand the assumptions of linear regression for accurate predictions.

Now, you're ready to apply linear regression to predict COVID-19 cases in Florida based on dates.

192. Building a customer churn prediction model

This is one of the most commonly asked Python interview questions: "How can you build a Keras sequential model to predict customer churn based on their tenure?"

To tackle this problem, we'll use Keras, a popular deep-learning framework in Python. Our goal is to predict customer churn based on the customer's tenure. Let's break down the steps:

STEP 1: IMPORT NECESSARY LIBRARIES

To get started, we need to import the essential libraries. These are like tools in your toolbox that we'll use throughout the process.

Program code:

```
from keras.models import Sequential
from keras.layers import Dense
from sklearn.metrics import confusion_matrix
```

STEP 2: BUILD THE SEQUENTIAL MODEL

Now, let's build the structure of our Keras sequential model. This is where the magic happens.

Program code:

```
model = Sequential()
model.add(Dense(12, input_dim=1, activation='relu'))
model.add(Dense(8, activation='relu'))
model.add(Dense(1, activation='sigmoid'))
```

Code explanation:

- We create a sequential model that lets us stack layers.
- We add a layer with 12 neurons, using `**relu**` (Rectified Linear Unit) activation and an input dimension of 1. The `**relu**` activation function is commonly used in hidden layers for better convergence.
- We add another layer with 8 neurons and `**relu**` activation.
- The final layer has 1 neuron with 'sigmoid' activation, perfect for binary classification tasks like customer churn prediction.

STEP 3: MODEL COMPILATION AND TRAINING

Now, it's time to compile our model and train it on our data. We specify the loss function, optimizer, and metrics to evaluate the model's performance.

Program code:

```
model.compile(loss='binary_crossentropy', optimizer='adam',
metrics=['accuracy'])
model.fit(x_train, y_train, epochs=150, validation_data=(x_test, y_test))
```

- `**loss='binary_crossentropy'**`: This is the loss function suitable for binary classification tasks like ours.
- `**optimizer='adam'**`: Adam is a popular optimization algorithm.
- `**metrics=['accuracy']** `: We'll measure the model's performance using accuracy.

STEP 4: MAKE PREDICTIONS

Once the model is trained, we can use it to make predictions on new data.

Program code:

```
y_pred = model.predict_classes(x_test)
```

STEP 5: EVALUATE THE MODEL

To understand how well our model is performing, we'll use a confusion matrix.

Program code:

```
confusion_matrix(y_test, y_pred)
```

Useful tips:

- Pay attention to the choice of activation functions. `**relu**` is a good default for hidden layers in most cases.
- The number of neurons in each layer can be adjusted based on your dataset and problem complexity.
- Experiment with different optimizers, as '**adam**' might not always be the best choice.

193. How to build a decision tree classification model with the iris dataset?

In this example, we'll create a decision tree classification model using the Iris dataset. Our goal is to predict the species of Iris flowers based on their sepal length. We'll walk through the code step by step, highlighting key points and providing explanations.

Program code:

```
# Import necessary libraries
from sklearn.model_selection import train_test_split
from sklearn.tree import DecisionTreeClassifier
from sklearn.metrics import confusion_matrix

# Extract the independent and dependent variables
y = iris[['Species']]
x = iris[['Sepal.Length']]

# Split the data into training and testing sets
x_train, x_test, y_train, y_test = train_test_split(x, y, test_size=0.4)

# Build the Decision Tree Classifier
dtc = DecisionTreeClassifier()
dtc.fit(x_train, y_train)

# Make predictions
y_pred = dtc.predict(x_test)

# Create a confusion matrix to evaluate the model
confusion_matrix_result = confusion_matrix(y_test, y_pred)
accuracy = (confusion_matrix_result[0, 0] + confusion_matrix_result[1, 1]
```

```
+ confusion_matrix_result[2, 2]) / (len(y_test))

  # Print the confusion matrix and accuracy
  print("Confusion Matrix:")
  print(confusion_matrix_result)
  print(f"Accuracy: {accuracy:.2f}")
```

Code explanation:

- We start by importing the necessary libraries for our model.
- We extract the independent variable (sepal length) and the dependent variable (Iris species) from the dataset.
- The data is divided into training and testing sets using the `**train_test_split**` function. This split is essential for evaluating the model's performance.
- We create a Decision Tree Classifier and fit it with the training data.
- We make predictions on the test data using the trained model.
- To assess the model's performance, we create a confusion matrix. The accuracy is calculated as the sum of correct predictions divided by the total number of test samples.

Following these steps, you can build a decision tree classification model for the Iris dataset and evaluate its accuracy. Remember to adjust hyperparameters and explore different evaluation metrics for more advanced analysis.

194. Build a decision tree regression model on the iris dataset

with "Petal length" as the independent variable and "Sepal length" as the dependent variable.

STEP 1: DATA PREPARATION

We start by selecting our independent variable (X) and dependent variable (y) from the iris dataset. In this case, we're using `**Petal.Length**` as X and `**Sepal.Length**` as y:

Program code:

```
x = iris[['Petal.Length']]
y = iris[['Sepal.Length']]
```

STEP 2: DATA SPLITTING

Next, we need to split our data into training and testing sets. This helps us evaluate the model's performance. We allocate 25% of the data for testing:

Program code:

```
from sklearn.model_selection import train_test_split

x_train, x_test, y_train, y_test = train_test_split(x, y, test_size=0.25)
```

STEP 3: BUILDING THE DECISION TREE REGRESSION MODEL

Now, we create a DecisionTreeRegressor and fit it with the training data:

Program code:

```
from sklearn.tree import DecisionTreeRegressor

dtr = DecisionTreeRegressor()
dtr.fit(x_train, y_train)
```

STEP 4: MAKING PREDICTIONS

With the model trained, we can make predictions on the test data:

Program code:

```
y_pred = dtr.predict(x_test)
```

STEP 5: EVALUATING THE MODEL

To assess the model's performance, we calculate the Mean Squared Error (MSE) between the actual and predicted values. Lower MSE indicates a better model:

Program code:

```
from sklearn.metrics import mean_squared_error

mse = mean_squared_error(y_test, y_pred)
```

What to pay attention to:

- Ensure you have the necessary libraries imported, such as `**sklearn**` and `**pandas**`.
- Double-check the column names used in your dataset (`**Petal.Length**` and `**Sepal.Length**` in this case).
- Adjust the `**test_size**` parameter in `**train_test_split**` as needed for your dataset.
- Understand that decision tree regression is used for continuous target variables.

Useful tips:

- Experiment with different regression models to find the best fit for your data.
- Visualize the decision tree to gain insights into its splitting criteria.

What to remember:
- Decision trees are a versatile tool for both classification and regression tasks.
- The Mean Squared Error (MSE) quantifies the model's prediction accuracy.

195. How will you scrape data from the website "cricbuzz"?

To scrape data from the `**cricbuzz**` website, you can use Python with the help of libraries like BeautifulSoup and requests. Here's a beginner-friendly example with practical tips:

Program code:
```
# Import necessary libraries
import sys
import time
from bs4 import BeautifulSoup
import requests

# Try to fetch the webpage
try:
    url = 'https://www.cricbuzz.com'  # Specify the URL you want to scrape
    page = requests.get(url)  # This might throw an exception if something
goes wrong.

except Exception as e:
    error_type, error_obj, error_info = sys.exc_info()  # Get the exception
information

    print('ERROR FOR LINK:', url)  # Print the link that caused the problem
    print(error_type, 'Line:', error_info.tb_lineno)  # Print error info and
line that threw the exception

    # You can choose to ignore this page and abandon it, or go back to the
previous page.

time.sleep(2)  # It's a good practice to add a delay to avoid overloading the
```

```
website.

    # Parse the webpage with BeautifulSoup
    soup = BeautifulSoup(page.text, 'html.parser')

    # Find specific elements on the page
    links = soup.find_all('span', attrs={'class': 'w_tle'})

    # Print the data you found
    for i in links:
        print(i.text)
        print("\n")
```

What to pay attention to:
- Ensure that you have the `**requests**` and `**BeautifulSoup**` libraries installed.
- Set the `**url**` variable to the specific webpage you want to scrape.
- Handle exceptions properly to avoid crashes.
- Include a delay (in this case, `**time.sleep(2)**`) to be polite to the website you're scraping.
- Adjust the `**soup.find_all**` method to target the HTML elements you need.

Useful tip:
- Always check the website's `**robots.txt**` file for scraping guidelines to avoid legal issues.

This code will help you get started with web scraping from `**cricbuzz**` or any other website of your choice.

196. Implementing the central limit theorem

Demonstrate the Central Limit Theorem using an `**insurance**` dataset and create two plots: `**Sampling Distribution of BMI**` and `**Population Distribution of BMI**`.

Program code:

```
# Import the necessary libraries and load the dataset
import pandas as pd
import numpy as np
import matplotlib.pyplot as plt
import seaborn as sns
```

```
df = pd.read_csv('insurance.csv')
series1 = df.charges

def central_limit_theorem(data, n_samples=1000, sample_size=500,
min_value=0, max_value=1338):
    """
    Use this function to demonstrate the Central Limit Theorem.

    Parameters:
        data - 1D array or pd.Series
        n_samples - number of samples to be created
        sample_size - size of each sample
        min_value - minimum index of the data
        max_value - maximum index value of the data
    """
    %matplotlib inline

    b = {}
    for i in range(n_samples):
        x = np.unique(np.random.randint(min_value, max_value,
size=sample_size))
        b[i] = data[x].mean()  # Mean of each sample

    c = pd.DataFrame()
    c['sample'] = b.keys()
    c['Mean'] = b.values()

    plt.figure(figsize=(15, 5))

    # Create the first subplot for Sampling Distribution of BMI
    plt.subplot(1, 2, 1)
    sns.distplot(c['Mean'])
    plt.title(f"Sampling Distribution of BMI\nμ = {round(c['Mean'].mean(),
3)} & SE = {round(c['Mean'].std(), 3)}")
    plt.xlabel('Data')
    plt.ylabel('Frequency')

    # Create the second subplot for Population Distribution of BMI
    plt.subplot(1, 2, 2)
    sns.distplot(data)
    plt.title(f"Population Distribution of BMI\nμ = {round(data.mean(), 3)} &
```

```
σ = {round(data.std(), 3)}")
        plt.xlabel('Data')
        plt.ylabel('Frequency')

        plt.show()

    # Execute the function with specified parameters
    central_limit_theorem(series1, n_samples=5000, sample_size=500)
```

Code explanation:

- We start by importing the insurance dataset using `**pd.read_csv('insurance.csv')**`.
- The `**central_limit_theorem**` function is defined with parameters for the data, the number of samples, sample size, minimum and maximum values.
- The necessary libraries like Pandas, NumPy, Matplotlib, and Seaborn are imported.
- The function generates samples, calculates their means, and stores the results in a DataFrame.
- Two subplots are created to visualize the Sampling Distribution of BMI and the Population Distribution of BMI.
- Key statistics such as mean (μ) and standard deviation (SE or σ) are displayed in the plot titles.
- The function is called with the insurance dataset and specified parameters to demonstrate the Central Limit Theorem.

This code helps you understand the Central Limit Theorem by visualizing how sample means tend to follow a normal distribution, even if the population distribution is not normal.

197. Write code to perform sentiment analysis on amazon reviews

Sentiment analysis on Amazon reviews is a common Python interview question.

Here's a step-by-step approach to tackle it, suitable for beginners. We'll provide practical code examples and tips along the way:

STEP 1: IMPORT NECESSARY LIBRARIES

Program code:

```
import pandas as pd
import numpy as np
import matplotlib.pyplot as plt
import tensorflow
from tensorflow.keras.preprocessing.text import Tokenizer,
text_to_word_sequence
from tensorflow.keras.preprocessing.sequence import pad_sequences
import bz2
from sklearn.metrics import f1_score, roc_auc_score, accuracy_score
import re
%matplotlib inline
```

STEP 2: LOAD AND PREPROCESS DATA

We'll load Amazon review data, preprocess it for analysis, and extract labels and texts.

Program code:

```
def get_labels_and_texts(file):
    labels = []
    texts = []
    for line in bz2.BZ2File(file):
        x = line.decode("utf-8")
        labels.append(int(x[9]) - 1)
        texts.append(x[10:].strip())
    return np.array(labels), texts

train_labels, train_texts = get_labels_and_texts('train.ft.txt.bz2')
test_labels, test_texts = get_labels_and_texts('test.ft.txt.bz2')
```

STEP 3: DATA PREPARATION

For simplicity, we'll work with a subset of the data to speed up the process.

Program code:

```
train_labels = train_labels[:500]
train_texts = train_texts[:500]
```

STEP 4: TEXT NORMALIZATION

Normalize the text by converting it to lowercase and removing non-alphanumeric characters.

Program code:

```
NON_ALPHANUM = re.compile(r'[\W]')
NON_ASCII = re.compile(r'[^a-z0-1\s]')

def normalize_texts(texts):
    normalized_texts = []
    for text in texts:
        lower = text.lower()
        no_punctuation = NON_ALPHANUM.sub(' ', lower)
        no_non_ascii = NON_ASCII.sub('', no_punctuation)
        normalized_texts.append(no_non_ascii)
    return normalized_texts

train_texts = normalize_texts(train_texts)
test_texts = normalize_texts(test_texts)
```

STEP 5: VECTORIZE TEXT DATA

We'll use Count Vectorization to convert text into a numerical format suitable for machine learning.

Program code:

```
from sklearn.feature_extraction.text import CountVectorizer
cv = CountVectorizer(binary=True)
cv.fit(train_texts)
X = cv.transform(train_texts)
X_test = cv.transform(test_texts)
```

STEP 6: TRAIN A LOGISTIC REGRESSION MODEL

Train a logistic regression model and tune the hyperparameter `**C**` to find the best accuracy.

Program code:

```
from sklearn.linear_model import LogisticRegression
from sklearn.model_selection import train_test_split

X_train, X_val, y_train, y_val = train_test_split(X, train_labels,
train_size=0.75)

for c in [0.01, 0.05, 0.25, 0.5, 1]:
    lr = LogisticRegression(C=c)
    lr.fit(X_train, y_train)
    print("Accuracy for C=%s: %s" % (c, accuracy_score(y_val,
```

```
lr.predict(X_val)))
```

STEP 7: PERFORM SENTIMENT ANALYSIS

Use the trained model to perform sentiment analysis on a sample review.

Program code:

```
prediction = lr.predict(X_test[29])
```

What to remember:

- To adapt this code for your specific dataset and further fine-tune the model for better results.

198. Creating a probability plot with NumPy and Matplotlib

In data analysis and statistics, probability plots are a valuable tool for visualizing the distribution of your data. In this example, we'll use NumPy and Matplotlib to create a probability plot.

STEP 1:

First, make sure you have the necessary libraries imported. Here, we'll need NumPy, MatplotLib, and SciPy:

Program code:

```
import numpy as np
import scipy.stats as stats
import matplotlib.pyplot as plt
```

STEP 2:

Generate some random data. We'll create two sets of data here. One with 1000 data points, normally distributed with a mean of 0 and a standard deviation of 1, and another with 100 data points, normally distributed with a mean of 20 and a standard deviation of 3:

Program code:

```
data1 = np.random.normal(loc=0, scale=1, size=1000)
data2 = np.random.normal(loc=20, scale=3, size=100)
```

STEP 3:

Calculate the percentiles of your data. You can use the `**np.percentile**` function to see how your data is distributed within the specified percentiles:

Program code:

```
percentiles_data1 = np.percentile(data1, 100)
```

STEP 4:

Create the probability plot. The `**stats.probplot**` function helps you visualize the distribution of your data. We'll use it with the `**norm**` distribution, which is the normal distribution. The `**plot**` argument is set to `**pylab**` for Matplotlib compatibility:

Program code:

```
stats.probplot(data2, dist="norm", plot=plt)
```

STEP 5:

Finally, display the probability plot using Matplotlib:

Program code:

```
plt.show()
```

Output:

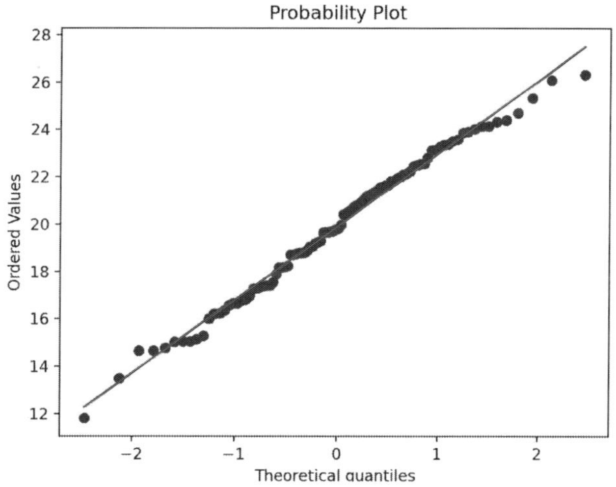

Useful tip:

- Experiment with different data distributions and sample sizes to gain a better understanding of probability plots and how they work.

What to remember:

- Probability plots are a handy way to assess the distribution of your data.
- Numpy, Scipy, and Matplotlib are useful libraries for data analysis and visualization.

Now, you're all set to create your probability plots and gain insights into your data's distribution!

199. Implement multiple linear regression on this iris dataset

The independent variables should be `**Sepal.Width**`, `**Petal.Length**`, `**Petal.Width**`, while the dependent variable should be `**Sepal.Length**`.

To implement multiple linear regression on the Iris dataset, follow these steps:

STEP 1: IMPORT THE NECESSARY LIBRARIES

Program code:

```
import pandas as pd
from sklearn.model_selection import train_test_split
from sklearn.linear_model import LinearRegression
from sklearn.metrics import mean_squared_error

# Load the Iris dataset
iris = pd.read_csv("iris.csv")
```

STEP 2: PREPARE THE DATA

Program code:

```
# Select independent and dependent variables
x = iris[['Sepal.Width', 'Petal.Length', 'Petal.Width']]
y = iris['Sepal.Length']
```

STEP 3: SPLIT THE DATA INTO TRAINING AND TESTING SETS

Program code:

```
x_train, x_test, y_train, y_test = train_test_split(x, y, test_size=0.35)
```

STEP 4: BUILD THE LINEAR REGRESSION MODEL

Program code:

```
lr = LinearRegression()
lr.fit(x_train, y_train)
y_pred = lr.predict(x_test)
```

STEP 5: CALCULATE THE MEAN SQUARED ERROR

Program code:

```
mse = mean_squared_error(y_test, y_pred)
```

STEP 6: INTERPRET THE RESULT

The mean squared error (MSE) measures the average squared difference between the actual Sepal.Length values and the predicted values by our model. Lower MSE indicates a better fit of the model to the data.

In this example, you've successfully implemented multiple linear regression on the Iris dataset to predict `**Sepal.Length**` based on `**Sepal.Width**`, `**Petal.Length**`, and `**Petal.Width**`.

What to remember:

- To adjust the dataset file path and explore other evaluation metrics if needed.

200. Analyzing credit fraud dataset

From credit fraud dataset find the percentage of transactions that are fraudulent and not fraudulent. Also build a logistic regression model, to find out if the transaction is fraudulent or not.

STEP 1: FIND PERCENTAGE OF FRAUDULENT TRANSACTIONS

First, let's calculate the percentage of fraudulent and non-fraudulent transactions in our credit fraud dataset.

Program code:

```
# Count non-fraudulent transactions
nfcount = len(data_df[data_df['Class'] == 0])

# Calculate the percentage of non-fraudulent transactions
percentage_not_fraud = (nfcount / len(data_df)) * 100

print("Percentage of non-fraudulent transactions in the dataset:",
percentage_not_fraud)

# Count fraudulent transactions
fcount = len(data_df[data_df['Class'] == 1])

# Calculate the percentage of fraudulent transactions
percentage_fraud = (fcount / len(data_df)) * 100

print("Percentage of fraudulent transactions in the dataset:",
percentage_fraud)
```

STEP 2: BUILD A LOGISTIC REGRESSION MODEL

Now, let's create a logistic regression model to predict whether a transaction is fraudulent or not.

Program code:

```
from sklearn.model_selection import train_test_split
from sklearn.linear_model import LogisticRegression
from sklearn import metrics

# Prepare the data
x = data_df.drop(['Class'], axis=1)  # Drop the target variable
y = data_df['Class']

# Split the data into training and testing sets
x_train, x_test, y_train, y_test = train_test_split(x, y, test_size=0.2,
random_state=42)

# Create and train the logistic regression model
logistic_reg = LogisticRegression()
logistic_reg.fit(x_train, y_train)
```

```
# Make predictions on the test data
y_pred = logistic_reg.predict(x_test)

# Calculate accuracy and confusion matrix
accuracy = logistic_reg.score(x_test, y_test)
confusion_matrix = metrics.confusion_matrix(y_test, y_pred)
print("Accuracy of the logistic regression model:", accuracy)
print("Confusion matrix:")
print(confusion_matrix)
```

Now, you can easily find the percentage of fraudulent and non-fraudulent transactions in your dataset and build a logistic regression model to predict fraud.

201. Implement a simple CNN on the MNIST dataset using Keras following this, also add drop-out layers

Implementing a Simple CNN on the MNIST Dataset with Dropout Layers

In this example, we'll create a Convolutional Neural Network (CNN) to classify handwritten digits from the MNIST dataset using Keras. We'll also include dropout layers to enhance the model's performance. Let's dive in:

Program code:

```
# Import necessary libraries
import numpy as np
import tensorflow as tf
from tensorflow.keras.datasets import mnist
from tensorflow.keras.models import Sequential
from tensorflow.keras.layers import Dense, Activation, Dropout, Flatten,
Reshape

from tensorflow.keras.layers import Convolution2D, MaxPooling2D
from tensorflow.keras import utils
import matplotlib.pyplot as plt
```

```
# Load and prepare the data
(x_train, y_train_num), (x_test, y_test_num) = mnist.load_data()
x_train = x_train.reshape(x_train.shape[0], 28, 28, 1).astype('float32')
x_test = x_test.reshape(x_test.shape[0], 28, 28, 1).astype('float32')
x_train /= 255
x_test /= 255
y_train = utils.to_categorical(y_train_num, 10)
y_test = utils.to_categorical(y_test_num, 10)
# Define the model
model = tf.keras.Sequential()

# Flatten images to vectors
model.add(Reshape((784,), input_shape=(28, 28, 1)))

# Add a dense layer with ReLU activation
model.add(Dense(128, kernel_initializer='he_normal', use_bias=True))
model.add(Activation("relu"))

# Add another dense layer for classification
model.add(Dense(10, kernel_initializer='he_normal', use_bias=True))
model.add(Activation("softmax"))

# Compile the model
model.compile(loss='categorical_crossentropy', optimizer='adam',
metrics=['accuracy'])

# Train the model
model.fit(x_train, y_train, epochs=1, batch_size=32,
validation_data=(x_test, y_test), verbose=1)

# Now, let's add dropout layers to improve the model's performance

# Define a new model
model_with_dropout = tf.keras.Sequential()

# 1st Convolutional Layer
model_with_dropout.add(Convolution2D(32, (3, 3), input_shape=(28, 28,
1)))
model_with_dropout.add(Activation('relu'))
```

```
# 2nd Convolutional Layer
model_with_dropout.add(Convolution2D(32, (3, 3)))
model_with_dropout.add(Activation('relu'))

# Max Pooling
model_with_dropout.add(MaxPooling2D(pool_size=(2, 2)))

# Dropout
model_with_dropout.add(Dropout(0.25))

# Fully Connected Layer
model_with_dropout.add(Flatten())
model_with_dropout.add(Dense(128))
model_with_dropout.add(Activation('relu'))

# More Dropout
model_with_dropout.add(Dropout(0.5))

# Prediction Layer
model_with_dropout.add(Dense(10))
model_with_dropout.add(Activation('softmax'))

# Compile the model
model_with_dropout.compile(loss='categorical_crossentropy',
optimizer='adam', metrics=['accuracy'])

# Train the model with dropout
model_with_dropout.fit(x_train, y_train, batch_size=32, epochs=1,
validation_data=(x_test, y_test), verbose=1)
```

With these dropout layers, you can enhance your model's ability to generalize and make better predictions. Remember to experiment with different hyperparameters to fine-tune your model for optimal results.

202. Building a popularity-based movie recommendation system

Popularity-based recommendation systems are a great starting point for understanding how recommendation systems work. In this example, we'll walk you through implementing one using

Python and the MovieLens dataset.

STEP 1: IMPORT THE NECESSARY LIBRARIES

Before we start, we need to import some essential libraries:

Program code:

```
import numpy as np
import pandas as pd
```

STEP 2: LOAD THE DATASET

We'll use two CSV files: `**ratings.csv**` and `**movies.csv**`. The first one contains user ratings, and the second one has movie details. Let's load them:

Program code:

```
ratings_data = pd.read_csv("ratings.csv")
movie_names = pd.read_csv("movies.csv")
```

STEP 3: MERGING DATA

Now, we'll merge the two datasets using the `**movieId**` column as the common key:

Program code:

```
movie_data = pd.merge(ratings_data, movie_names, on='movieId')
```

STEP 4: CALCULATE MOVIE RATINGS

To recommend popular movies, we'll calculate the mean and count of ratings for each movie title. This helps us identify which movies are highly rated and frequently rated. Here's how to do it:

Program code:

```
# Calculate the mean rating for each movie
movie_mean_ratings = movie_data.groupby('title')['rating'].mean()

# Sort movies by mean rating in descending order (most popular)
top_rated_movies = movie_mean_ratings.sort_values(ascending=False)

# Count the number of ratings for each movie
movie_rating_counts = movie_data.groupby('title')['rating'].count()

# Combine the mean ratings and rating counts into a DataFrame
ratings_mean_count = pd.DataFrame({'mean_rating': movie_mean_ratings,
```

```
'rating_count': movie_rating_counts})
```

STEP 5: EXPLORE THE RESULTS

Now, let's take a look at the top-rated and most frequently rated movies:

Program code:

```
    # Print the top-rated movies
    print("Top-Rated Movies:")
    print(top_rated_movies.head())

    # Print the most frequently rated movies
    print("Most Frequently Rated Movies:")
    print(ratings_mean_count.sort_values(by='rating_count',
ascending=False).head())
```

By following these steps, you've created a simple popularity-based movie recommendation system. It's a great starting point for understanding the basics of recommendation systems. In the real world, you can enhance this approach with more complex algorithms, but this is a beginner-friendly introduction to the topic. Have fun exploring and experimenting with different datasets and recommendation techniques!

203. How to implement Naive Bayes algorithm on the diabetes dataset?

Naive Bayes is a popular algorithm for classification tasks. In this example, we'll use it to predict whether a person has diabetes or not using the diabetes dataset. We'll guide you through the steps with clear explanations and code snippets.

STEP 1: IMPORT NECESSARY LIBRARIES

First, we need to import the libraries we'll be using. These libraries will help us handle and visualize the data effectively.

Program code:

```
import numpy as np
import pandas as pd
import matplotlib.pyplot as plt
import seaborn as sns
from sklearn.model_selection import train_test_split
from sklearn.naive_bayes import GaussianNB
from sklearn import metrics

%matplotlib inline

pdata = pd.read_csv("pima-indians-diabetes.csv")
```

STEP 2: EXPLORE THE DATA

Before building the Naive Bayes model, it's essential to understand the dataset. We can start by plotting histograms for the first 8 columns to see the data's distribution:

Program code:

```
columns = list(pdata)[0:-1]
pdata[columns].hist(stacked=False, bins=100, figsize=(12, 30), layout=(14,
2))
```

If you want to explore the correlations between features visually, use the `**plot_corr**` function:

Program code:

```
def plot_corr(df, size=11):
    corr = df.corr()
    fig, ax = plt.subplots(figsize=(size, size))
    ax.matshow(corr)
    plt.xticks(range(len(corr.columns)), corr.columns)
    plt.yticks(range(len(corr.columns)), corr.columns)

plot_corr(pdata)
```

STEP 3: PREPARE THE DATA

Next, we'll prepare the data for training the Naive Bayes model. We'll split the dataset into predictor features and the predicted class:

Program code:

```
X = pdata.drop('class', axis=1)  # Predictor feature columns
Y = pdata['class']  # Predicted class (1=True, 0=False)
```

Now, split the data into training and testing sets:

Program code:

```
x_train, x_test, y_train, y_test = train_test_split(X, Y, test_size=0.3,
random_state=1)
```

STEP 4: BUILD AND TRAIN THE MODEL

We'll create a Gaussian Naive Bayes model and train it using the training data:

Program code:

```
diab_model = GaussianNB()
diab_model.fit(x_train, y_train.ravel())
```

STEP 5: EVALUATE THE MODEL

After training the model, it's time to evaluate its performance. We'll check the model's accuracy on both the training and testing data:

Program code:

```
diab_train_predict = diab_model.predict(x_train)
print("Training Model Accuracy:
{0:.4f}".format(metrics.accuracy_score(y_train, diab_train_predict)))

diab_test_predict = diab_model.predict(x_test)
print("Testing Model Accuracy:
{0:.4f}".format(metrics.accuracy_score(y_test, diab_test_predict))
```

STEP 6: CONFUSION MATRIX

Lastly, we can visualize the model's performance using a confusion matrix:

Program code:

```
cm = metrics.confusion_matrix(y_test, diab_test_predict, labels=[1, 0])
df_cm = pd.DataFrame(cm, index=["1", "0"], columns=["Predict 1", "Predict
0"])
plt.figure(figsize=(7, 5))
sns.heatmap(df_cm, annot=True)
```

This confusion matrix helps us understand how well our model predicts diabetes.

What to remember:

- To import the necessary libraries, explore the data, prepare it for training, build the model, and evaluate its performance. This example will help you get started with implementing the Naive Bayes algorithm for classification tasks.

Acknowledgments

I want to thank the fantastic individuals who have made **"How to Crack the Coding Interview Fun?"** possible. This book is a testament to the collective effort and support of those who have been part of this incredible journey.

I want to express my most profound appreciation to Taras – his expertise and dedication have been invaluable throughout the creation of this book. Your insights, meticulous reviews, and feedback have enriched the content and made it exceptional.

My beloved wife, Alla, has been my unwavering source of support, patience, and encouragement. Her belief in my abilities and loving encouragement kept me going during late nights of writing.

To you, my dear readers, I'm genuinely thankful. Your interest in this book and your dedication to mastering Python have been a driving force behind my passion for creating a resource that serves your needs.

This book is a labor of love made possible by these exceptional individuals. I am deeply grateful for the impact they've had on my writing journey.

To Alla and Taras and all of you, I owe a debt of gratitude that can never be repaid. Your belief in me has given me the strength to push boundaries and strive for greatness.

As you explore the pages of **"How to Crack the Coding Interview Fun?"**, I hope you feel the warmth and admiration I've poured into every question, answer, and explanation. May this book become your steadfast companion in your quest for Python excellence, just as your unwavering support has been for me.

I WILL BE PLEASED IF THIS BOOK HELPS IN YOUR LIFE!

Oliver

Printed in Great Britain
by Amazon

34815198R00137